CHANGEMAKING

Richard Bevan

CHANGEMAKING

Tactics and Resources
for Managing Organizational Change

ChangeStart
PRESS

Publisher's Cataloging-in-Publication Data

Bevan, Richard
Changemaking: Tactics and Resources for Managing Organizational Change

ISBN-13: 978-1449969981
ISBN-10: 1449969984
BISAC: Business & Economics | Management
Managing change; change management tools; leadership; communication; listening

For information contact ChangeStart Press, Seattle, WA | info@changestart.com

Printed in the USA by CreateSpace
Available from Amazon.com and other retailers
or from https://www.createspace.com/3418532

Cover design by Bill Greaves, Concept West
Author photograph by Lesley Burvill-Holmes

Using this book

Changemaking is about the details of planning and managing change. Focusing on tactics rather than strategy, the book is for those who carry out the practical day-to-day work of supporting and sustaining change.

Instead of case studies of large-scale strategy, the book uses short case histories (readily identifiable by use of a different typeface). These illustrate what can go wrong and how it can be made to go right. The aim is to provide not just ideas and guidance, but also materials that you can refer to, draw on, and adapt as you develop methods and processes for managing change in your own organization.

The first section of each chapter contains guidance, ideas, and cases. This material is followed by a series of resources based on tools developed and used over many years of consulting, leading, and teaching. Browse these checklists, templates, tactics, FAQs, talking points, and e-mails. Select and adapt those that are relevant to your work responding to and managing change. The tools are identified, and separated from the main text, by a shaded heading at the top of each resource page.

Change doesn't always go smoothly. Often, it runs into difficulties. These may include unanticipated questions from those involved; uncertainty among managers trying to implement a new organization or business model; resistance to new structures or roles.

Accordingly, after Chapter 1 provides an overview of the issue and challenge, and a framework for managing change, Chapter 2 answers the often-posed question, "If a change isn't working out well, how can we get it back on track?"

Chapters 3 through 6 examine specific processes and techniques. Chapter 7 provides a brief restatement of the core factors for successful change, and examples of tactics to address issues and challenges.

Feedback, comments, and ideas will be truly welcome. Please send them to info@changestart.com.

Contents

1. Seeking and facilitating change

2. Keeping change on track

3. Making the case for change

4. Managing employee focus groups

5. Developing and managing a change planning workshop

6. Developing FAQ guides

7. At a glance

CHAPTER 1

Seeking and facilitating change

MORE EASILY SAID THAN DONE

Most people manage change continually: at home, in recreation and volunteer activities, and at work. They have an intuitive understanding of what needs to happen if change is to move forward. Even if they haven't consciously thought about or documented the principles, they do what makes sense. They consult people, discuss the alternatives, try to anticipate and plan around the obstacles, adapt their plans as needed, take action, and address issues and challenges along the way.

Yet when organizations implement change, these straightforward steps are often missed. The intent and the broad strategy get the attention; the details of execution are forgotten.

The elements of effective change are simple: be clear about purpose and process; listen to and involve stakeholders; provide needed resources; align systems and processes to support the change; lead with clarity and involvement; communicate relentlessly; track progress; follow up; and course-correct. That's it. But while it's easy to say, it usually proves very hard to do.

Good news . . . and bad
The good news is that the core factors are well-known and readily followed. The bad news is that, in the pressure of ongoing business activity, they're often forgotten.

Many major change initiatives struggle, and they often fail.[1] In part, this is because implementation is through some version of the "memo-and-conference-call" approach: announce the change, trust that those involved will quickly learn and adapt—and

---

1. For example, two-thirds or more of Total Quality Management (TQM) programs and re-engineering initiatives fail, according to Peter Senge et al. in *The Dance of Change* (New York: Doubleday, 1999). And according to John P. Kotter in *Leading Change* (Boston: Harvard Business School Press, 1996), few of the companies studied were successful in making major changes to their ways of doing business.

hope for the best. Smaller-scale changes also encounter unexpected resistance and very often prove far more challenging than the sponsors anticipate.

The emphasis may be on the strategic purpose of the change ("the merger offers the opportunity for significant synergies leading to cost savings"; or, "this acquisition fills an important gap in our product range") with insufficient attention paid to making it happen.

So the good news is that the core factors are well-known and straightforward. The bad news is that these principles are often forgotten or ignored amid the pressure of ongoing business operations.

The goal is to have the transition—or transaction—occur smoothly, with minimal disruption and maximum support. In practice, though, change is often not well planned or managed. The result can be costly, ranging from a temporary loss of focus on customers to large-scale failure in integrating two organizations.

CORE FACTORS IN SUCCESSFUL CHANGE MANAGEMENT

These seven factors summarize the conditions, resources, and processes that support successful change.

- *Clarity:* Be clear and unambiguous about the purpose of the change, its direction, and the approach.
- *Engagement:* Build a sense of ownership and commitment; consult with and involve the people who will be affected by the change.
- *Resources:* Put in place the needed resources (e.g., financial, human, technical) to enable the change.
- *Alignment:* Ensure that systems and processes (e.g., rewards, information, accounting, training) support the change.
- *Leadership:* Guide, train, and equip leaders at every level so that they display consistent commitment to the change.
- *Communication:* Ensure an effective two-way flow of information; be aware of issues and questions; provide timely responses.
- *Tracking:* Establish clear goals; assess progress against these; adjust and fine-tune as necessary.

MAKING IT HAPPEN

"Everyone knows you have to do these things" is a frequent comment when the core factors or principles of successful change management are outlined. But when we ask if those principles have been put into practice, it often turns out that perhaps some of the details were overlooked; maybe most of the details; sometimes, all of them.[2] In many change initiatives, large-scale and small, at least one of these principles (and often several of them) are not followed.

We often hear senior leaders say of their employees, "They're smart; they'll figure it out." And yes, they are indeed smart. They figure out that the direction isn't clear and the planning is imperfect. They figure out that they need a great deal more convincing that this is a change they want to be aligned with and involved in.

The details are what make change work for the people whom it impacts most sharply. It's hard work to make a significant additional effort while continuing to run a complex business. But there's a high price if that effort is not sustained. Employees get distracted and demotivated; customers' needs get ignored or forgotten; and managers are consumed by questions, issues, concerns, and distractions.[3]

Change can happen without all seven core factors in place. But it's likely to be difficult, expensive, and painful—for your customers as well as your employees.

CAN CHANGE BE MANAGED?

It's been said that change happens and can't be managed. There is a valid point in the assertion: the ongoing evolution of technology, business practices, and economic change can certainly sweep organizations along with them. But while some organizations may be passengers or followers rather than leaders, others are seeking and creating change, and building success on that commitment.

This book asserts that the way change takes effect, and the way it influences the state of the business and its ability to serve its customers, can and should be managed. People can be informed, consulted, and engaged—or not. Systems can be adapted and aligned with new ways of doing business—or not. Leaders can actively communicate, listen, and

---

2. The set of core factors listed here aligns with models and frameworks developed by many writers, educators, and leaders. For examples, see John P. Kotter, *Leading Change*, Boston: Harvard Business School Press, 1996, and Daryl R. Conner, *Managing at the Speed of Change*, New York: Random House, 1992. The challenge doesn't lie in understanding the process, or even in putting together a plan. It's in putting the plan into action and sustaining the effort.
3. Ram and Colvin, "Why CEOs Fail" (*Fortune*, June 21, 1999).

persuade—or not. Through these and other processes, change can be successfully planned, shaped, and implemented.

Daryl Conner views change as a shift or disruption in expectations.[4] And when expectations change—especially if they change in a negative way—people react by seeking to regain or retain the circumstances that were in place and with which they were comfortable. They may be open to change, and often see (at the front line) the reasons that are driving it. But they need to know that it's appropriate and well-planned. Behavior that's interpreted as resistance may be an effort to understand and learn.

Change has patterns that can be anticipated, reflecting typical reactions of individuals and groups. The pace and nature of adaptation is strongly influenced by the way change is managed, or by the way leaders explain, direct, support, and assess the process.

Whether change is initiated by the organization (installation of new systems, a merger, a new organizational structure, appointment of a new CEO) or is forced on the organization (new competitive behaviors, technological redundancy, government regulations, a hostile takeover) leaders can respond in ways that ignore and increase resistance, or in ways that understand and address it.

Some business leaders create change; others respond. But all have to manage it.

SOURCES OF RESISTANCE AND SUPPORT

People are not intrinsically averse to change. Indeed, employees seek change as much as leaders do. Employees are sometimes more aware than leaders of poor product quality, unresponsive service, long wait times, or fast and effective competitors. They see it and hear about it every day.

As a telecommunications engineer who was laying fiber-optic cable in a new service area said, "We see competitors out there all the time, just like us. We have to do it better and faster. When the CEO says employees 'don't get it,' I wonder where he's been for the last few years."

But for all that employees see and understand what's happening on the front lines, they need control and certainty. They want resources, information, and support. They want job security and development opportunities. They want to be part of a responsive, successful business.

---

4. Daryl R. Conner, *Managing at the Speed of Change* (New York: Random House, 1992).

Sometimes, leaders become detached from this day-to-day reality. Many organizational cultures value stability; their leaders find comfort in the status quo and lead change with less than full commitment. They may receive generous rewards even if the company goes under. Leaders who say that employees "don't get it" may be seriously underestimating the awareness of the audience; or perhaps they themselves have failed to observe and learn.

Why resist change?

Resistance to change arises from many causes. Most are reasonable and rational—but also addressable. Here are just a few:

- *Comfort with the status quo:* "I like my present office."
- *Threat to security:* "How am I going to pay the mortgage?"
- *Loss of control:* "This is being done to me, no one asked me about it, and I can't influence it."
- *Shifted expectations:* "They told us we'd be getting new furniture, and they just brought over the old stuff."
- *Failure to convince:* "I've got a better idea."
- *Lack of trust, or negative history:* "That's just what they said last time; it's the same old story."
- *Concern about results:* "My customers aren't going to like this, and I agree with them."
- *Work pressure:* "I just can't take on anything else."
- *Discomfort with learning new skills:* "We've always done it this way; I don't know how to do it differently."
- *Lack of familiarity:* "Why did they move the copier?"

Why support change?

Here are some of the many reasons that people support, seek, and celebrate change:

- *Personal growth:* "I can learn from this."
- *Ambition:* "I want a career here, so I'll make the move."
- *Loyalty, trust, commitment:* "I believe them; I want to help make it work; I want us to succeed."
- *Personal gain:* "I'm going to be able to earn more."
- *Self-preservation:* "I need to do this if I want to keep my job."

- *Conviction:* "I know what's happening out there; we have to do this to keep up with the competition."
- *Involvement:* "It's my idea; I'm going to make it work."
- *Adventure:* "This could be fun."

Supported change requires that the net impact of these forces supports the new direction, system, or structure. Managing change involves discovering prevailing beliefs, concerns, and feelings; taking action to reinforce the positives and address the negatives; and bringing them into a favorable balance.

When you encounter resistance to change, it's important and useful to understand the reason for that resistance. It may be emotional rather than rational; it may be based on inaccurate perceptions about the change and its impact; it may be based on relationships and personalities; it may be based on self-interest. Whatever the reason, understanding it is the key to creating conditions in which resistance can be addressed and redirected or overcome.

A hard lesson of change management is that the process of building buy-in very often takes discussion, experience, conversation, evidence, and reinforcement—among just a few of the levers or processes through which opinions form or change. And applying these "levers of persuasion" to build buy-in takes time. That, in part, is why the memo-and-conference-call approach so often runs into resistance. It doesn't allow sufficiently for the process of learning and adaptation. Those involved want to understand, be heard, and be involved and respected. They want to be part of the conversation and not passive bystanders—or, as they might see it, victims.

START BY LISTENING

If it were possible to condense the key to successfully managing change into a single word, that word would be *listen*—to employees, customers, managers, business partners, vendors, and whoever else has a stake in the issue or the outcome. If you're involved in change—especially if you're responsible for making it happen—you must continually ask yourself, "What do the people involved think and feel and need right now? If I asked them, what would they say? And have they got ideas about how to make this change happen more effectively?"

If you don't know the answers to these questions, there's an easy and obvious course of action: go out and get them. This exploration can be done quickly and effectively. You can learn a great deal in informal conversations in the course of day-to-day business; or you can plan and conduct a more rigorous assessment. Whatever the method, you learn what's going right and wrong; the people you engage in the discussion learn that someone cares and is listening; and that their feelings are respected and their ideas are needed.

So consider who will be most affected; ask questions; listen carefully to the responses. This can be on a small, local scale—informal conversations. Or it can be on a large, corporate-wide scale, through meetings, surveys, or focus groups. It can be through social media, using blogs and other interactive forums, including the rapidly growing set of tools and resources that are part of what has become known as Web 2.0.

You'll learn fast; you'll have answers to your own questions; and you'll have raw material for a plan to address issues, correct problems, or lead the change.

Along with listening comes sustained follow-up. Is the change working? What needs to happen to make it work better? What's working well and what's not? What are people thinking and feeling? What were the unintended consequences, and how can they be addressed?

Formal and informal research into the nature of change provides data indicating that few significant change efforts proceed as smoothly or rapidly as their sponsors hope and expect. For example, a 1995 *Business Week*/Mercer study of 150 mergers found that about half reduced shareholder value relative to broad market indexes, and another third contributed only marginally.[5]

Of course, mergers may fail—and many do—for reasons other than the way the integration is managed. If the strategic or tactical framework is invalid or weak, then even the most effective change management process will be unable to create a strong result. But effective change management, supporting a sound strategy and direction, will address the challenges, distractions and costs, and raise the likelihood that the goals are achieved.

While obstacles and issues might be routinely expected, their number and extent often takes change sponsors by surprise. So assess pro-

---

5. "The Case Against Mergers" (*Business Week* Special Report, October 30, 1995).

gress; fix it; keep listening, learning, and leading. Never assume that things will happen as planned. In short, don't assume a good outcome or hope for one: focus on the process and *make* it work.

Case history: Validate the assumptions

A midsized company that developed and sold accounting and sales-management software acquired a small business, headquartered in another state. The acquired business was in the same field, with a special focus on payroll-related products. The acquisition neatly filled a significant gap in the product range of the acquirer. A task force was working on integration issues including pay systems, reporting relationships, office consolidation, and software platforms.

A team member suggested that the integration team hold meetings with developers in both organizations. The divisional VP's response was, "We don't need to waste their time; we know what they think. Work with the managers. We can't afford to take anyone else off the job."

Work to integrate development teams was starting, but much was conducted by senior managers team of the two organizations, and mostly behind closed doors. Concerns soon began to surface:

- ♦ Software developers in the acquiring company discovered that their current pay rates were significantly less than those in the acquired business. They received stock options and other benefits, but saw the other group as well ahead on current pay.
- ♦ Rumors included a supposed plan for a cost-saving relocation of development teams to the acquired organization's out-of-state office.
- ♦ Since the two groups worked 800 miles apart, neither learned much about the other except through brief glimpses of managers visiting to work on transition issues.

Distraction took its toll: productivity fell sharply; customer issues took longer to resolve; managers weren't available to assist, guide, or rebuild focus. Matters came to a head when a lead developer submitted his resignation. As he told his manager, "This merger was the last straw. I'm not going to stick around to see these new guys taking over, being paid more, and getting credit for what we've done here."

The manager was stunned: "They're not taking over—far from it. We do expect that a couple of their stronger managers will get team leader roles, but that's good for everyone. And we'll be bringing them onto our pay scale—we just have to work out the details."

The VP listened to these and many other accounts of concerns, issues, and resistance. It was time to rethink some faulty assumptions: that people would accept the situation, focus on their work, and figure things out; that change would be welcomed, along with an injection of new talent; that the details of integration would be quickly and effectively resolved. Above all, it was time to revisit the assumption that the businesses' leaders "knew what people were thinking."

Seeking a more proactive approach, the VP formed a team to work on strengthening communication and involvement. The goal was to communicate better, listen more, and address the instinctive reactions (and often resistance) of those involved in change who don't have all the facts.

The new team developed a variety of tactics, starting with town-hall-style meetings at both locations. At these, the VP opened with an acknowledgment that the process needed to engage people in a much more active way. Following are other tactics the team suggested:

- Implement a brief online survey, administered monthly, to gather reactions and input.
- Hold weekly progress meetings.
- Establish small groups to plan and monitor details of the integration process.
- Establish a blog to provide updates on issues, obstacles, and progress, and invite input, comment, and ideas.
- Set up exchange visits to help employees get to know the other company's culture, work processes, and people.
- Form an advisory group of senior developers.

The early going was rough, with negative research results, passive meeting participants, and continued resistance. But the process was moving back on track. In the following months, concerns were identified and addressed, trust increased, communication began to flow effectively, and the benefits of synergy and collaboration became apparent in new features and improved product performance.

APPLYING THE FRAMEWORK

The set of seven core factors described in this chapter (clarity, engagement, resources, alignment, leadership, communication, and tracking) provide a framework in which change can be successfully managed. The factors serve as criteria for assessing the status and nature of the change, and identifying areas where action or resources are needed.

In the following chapters, the framework will be apparent in assessment tools, in suggestions for actions and processes to support change, and in other contexts. It can serve as a reminder about areas where planning and action—and ongoing review and maintenance—are likely to be needed to sustain the effort effectively.

And if a change initiative has run into difficulties, the framework can help you diagnose the area or areas where effort is needed to get the process back on track.

It's an apparent paradox that leaders seek change, and so do employees, and yet leaders often encounter resistance; and employees (and other stakeholders) express frustration with progress and support.

An effective strategy for change responds to stakeholder expectations and concerns; identifies areas of conflict and opportunity and addresses them; and builds trust and solutions by involving and engaging those with a stake in the outcome.

CHAPTER 2

Keeping change on track

PITFALLS: WHY DOES CHANGE GO OFF THE RAILS?

Change within organizations frequently evolves in unpredictable and unsatisfactory ways. There are countless potential pitfalls. Unintended consequences abound.

Even in change efforts that are well-planned and well-executed, people have a natural tendency to ask questions and to analyze purpose and implications—especially if they haven't been involved in the planning. This can slow down the process and create challenges and additional workload. But it can also provide insight and information about how best to manage the process.

Following are a few of the pitfalls that cause change to get off-track:

- Managers communicate a case for change that is unrealistic or incomplete; it isn't readily understood.
- The costs of implementing and supporting change are not adequately acknowledged or planned for.
- Leaders assume they know what people think. They fail to identify key concerns and obstacles.
- Training or other support—including resources to assist with the workload of those involved in planning and managing the transition—is limited or nonexistent.
- Existing systems (e.g., rewards, training, information) don't support the new model.
- Leaders expect to persuade and inform by one-way communication. Their audiences have limited opportunity to ask questions, offer ideas, or engage in discussion about the changes.
- Communication about the change is too lengthy, unfocused, or detailed to command attention, comprehension, and buy-in.

21

- Managers don't support the direction and approach.
- Leaders fail to address dissent from individuals or groups who do not respond to efforts to inform and engage them.[6]
- Input, questions, and ideas aren't recorded and documented. As a result, responses and tactics don't reflect the needs.
- The organization relies on only one communication method (e.g., e-mail) to convey information about complex changes.
- Leaders make a premature assumption of success and fail to follow up, support, and drive continuing change.

Awareness of these and other pitfalls doesn't ensure success. But it does provide ideas about where change most often gets off track, and opportunities to implement course corrections. Each pitfall has a positive counterpart—a proactive measure to support and facilitate change. This book discusses many of these pitfalls and proactive tactics. Resource 2.11 (page 60) consolidates and lists them.

BUILD PLANNING ON AN UNDERSTANDING OF THE ISSUES

At its simplest level, keeping change on track involves understanding the reasons for resistance, concern, or slow progress; and then addressing those issues. For example:

- If sales reps are displaying a high level of anxiety and results are falling short of goals, ask them why. Perhaps they're uncomfortable with the new product line and need training and education.
- If customer service standards are sliding, ask customers and service staff what's happening. Perhaps the pressure to hold costs down is forcing reductions in contact time and encouraging staff to end calls before the customer is fully satisfied.
- If employees are challenging managers with issues and concerns, they're probably missing information, or haven't yet had a chance to ask questions or offer ideas. Managers may not be equipped with clear responses.

---

6. Sometimes an individual who resists change for personal, historical, or economic reasons may not be successfully engaged through enquiry, conversation, involvement, or leadership. There are circumstances where it may be best for the organization to move such an individual elsewhere in the organization—or out of it.

- If strongly performing employees are reluctant to accept supervisory roles, find out why. There may be issues with pay, training, or career development. Employees may feel that they won't be rewarded, or that they don't have the experience, or that promotion might mean loss of overtime without gains in compensation.

The simple tactic of exploring issues at their source is a powerful tool for redirecting change initiatives. ("Let's find out how things are going, what's on their minds, and what's causing the concerns; then let's address the issues.")

Crises can fulfill a useful forcing function. They encourage change sponsors to rethink the purpose and direction of change, and to address with more care the needs of the various stakeholders involved. And while it might have been preferable if the issues had been anticipated, learning from setbacks may help the organization do things better the next time around.

> **Track questions and seek responses**
> Document questions from stakeholders. Seek responses from those familiar with the issues.

A plan for corrective action can be based on an analysis of where the change is off track, what issues have developed, and what needs have become apparent.

Case history: Getting change back on track

A specialized athletic-equipment company decided to reorganize its sales force. The process had seemed straightforward and routine:

- Six new regions were created; 32 existing areas, along with four newly created ones, would report to these regions.
- To direct regional activity, six area managers moved up to become regional leaders. Selection was already in progress for the open area manager positions that these moves created.
- Some reps would be asked to relocate to maintain customer coverage; many accounts would be reassigned based on leadership and location changes.
- The executive directing the change, the VP for marketing and sales, sent a detailed e-mail describing the changes to all managers and asked them to pass on the details to their teams.

Customers were notified of the changes by e-mail. Meetings and other follow-up steps were left to the discretion of managers in the field.

Unintended consequences abounded:

- Within days of the announcement, regional managers were reporting uncertainty, discontent, and push-back among the sales force.
- Many employees asked their managers how they could compete for one of the new positions.
- Customers who read about the changes in the press were calling to ask what it meant.
- Account managers feared they would lose key relationships and sought guidance on what to say to their customers.

"It's not as complex as they think," commented the VP. "It's just a simple reorg with a few changes in location and role. Can't they figure it out for themselves?"

The negative reactions were typical responses to change, but most could have been precluded with a few simple preventive actions.

- There were answers to all the questions, but nobody had prepared and distributed those ahead of time.
- There was a clear process for selecting new managers, but it hadn't been communicated.
- While there was no customer communication plan, it wouldn't have been hard to put one in place.

Now the organization was dealing with a high level of anxiety and loss of focus on the business. A simple set of changes with positive outcomes for almost all those involved (no job losses; plenty of opportunities for growth) hadn't been clearly and thoughtfully communicated.

The VP decided it was necessary to go back to the drawing board. He assembled a small, multilevel team and asked members to spend two days in an intensive review of stakeholder concerns and questions. The goal was to develop responses and create an appropriate action plan.

The planning effort was better late than never. The team formulated a set of appropriate plans:

- An e-mail from the VP went to everyone in the sales organization. It clearly described the purpose and nature of the changes and was accompanied by a comprehensive FAQ guide.[7]
- Every region held conference calls with area managers and sales reps to follow up and answer questions.
- All employees with direct customer contact received a template for customer communication, including talking points.
- An internal Web page was established where people could post additional questions and read responses.
- Managers were asked to monitor reactions among their teams.
- Issues, ideas, and information were shared in a weekly conference call facilitated by the VP.

The concerns diminished as more and better information was shared. Employees and managers adapted to the changes. But the cost had been high in loss of focus, wasted time, missed customer opportunities, and increased employee anxiety.

Better to get it right the first time.

A FRAMEWORK FOR FOCUSING CHANGE

In the balance of this chapter, a process is outlined for assessing the status of your change initiative, identifying the challenges, and implementing corrective action.[8] Starting on page 48, you'll find a variety of materials to help you manage the process. These materials include stakeholder assessment guides, communication tactics, meeting agendas, evaluation templates, and checklists.

Source documents and models can't cover every situation or need. The guidance and tools in this chapter offer starting points. The resources can save time and contribute to your thinking and planning, but need to be adapted for the specifics of your own situation.

---

7. Frequently Asked Questions—see Chapter 6 (starting on page 165) for more information about FAQ development and application.
8. The process describes how you could work with a team; but, if you're working on your own, the sequence of steps and the resources are still relevant.

To refocus change and get it back on track, you need to select people to work with you; assess progress; identify issues and obstacles; gather input from key stakeholders; and use the findings to develop tactics.

If you're in a small organization, or working on a local change, perhaps your team will have only one or two other members. In a larger organization, or where the change involves many people and significant resources, you will want to put together a diverse team. This team will share the workload, develop creative ideas, engage with stakeholders, and work with the organization's leadership.

Here are the phases. Each is described in more detail in the material that follows. If you are familiar with the process—or have one of your own that you prefer to follow—you can skip this section and go directly to the tools and templates starting on page 48.

Phase 1: Form a team

- Identify team members: look for individuals (e.g., managers, sales reps, HR staff) who have knowledge of and insight into the change process.
- Invite participants: define the purpose, outline the time commitment, and describe the process and expected outcome.
- Bring the team together: lay the groundwork, clarify roles and timeline, and begin work on the project.

Phase 2: Identify and document the issues

- Make an initial evaluation of key issues and obstacles, and the impact the change will have on business processes and results.
- Assess the status of the change by formulating questions built around the core factors.
- Identify areas where more data and assessments may be needed.

Phase 3: Gather input from stakeholders

- Identify stakeholders, including those most involved, most affected by the outcome, and/or most able to influence the process and results.
- Collect input from these individuals and groups on results, issues, questions, and ideas.

- Combine this feedback with the results of your initial assessment to provide a complete picture of the status of the change effort and the key issues that need to be resolved.

Phase 4: Develop tactics and take action

- Review the data and develop plans for addressing issues and responding to questions.
- Identify resources, responsibilities, and timing.
- Share the resulting plans with leadership and others; amend and fine-tune as necessary; begin to implement.

Phase 5: Assess progress and course-correct

- Monitor progress by evaluating results against business goals, and by continuing to seek stakeholder input.
- Apply course corrections as needed.

PHASE 1: FORM A TEAM

A small team of key people involved in the change effort can collaborate to evaluate progress, identify issues and obstacles, and plan and direct corrective action. You need input and guidance from people who have a good understanding of the change and of the people involved.

The team can help ensure that you accurately and completely assess the situation, target the right people and groups to take part in research, and develop plans that will address the issues and needs.

> **What if I'm the only person working on this?**
> If yours is a small organization or if the change initiative is limited in extent, you may be planning and driving it single-handedly. The process will still apply, and you can validate your approach by sharing findings with key managers and asking for comments and guidance.

Identify team members

The scale and nature of the change may determine who and how many people you engage for your team.

Enlist a diverse range of perspectives to increase the effectiveness of your team. Engage people from different functions and locations to review findings and provide input for getting change back on track.

You might include:

- Managers whose operations are affected by the change.
- Individuals with special awareness of key stakeholder groups, such as HR staff dealing with issues arising from a plant closure.
- Representatives from corporate communications who are managing public and/or internal reactions to the change.
- People with knowledge or skills that are especially relevant, such as Information Technology (IT) professionals if the issue is related to IT systems.

An extended virtual team can be a useful source of quick reviews and input.[9] Members of this group won't need to take part in meetings, can respond via e-mail at a time of their choosing, and may need to commit only a few minutes of time. But they increase your organizational reach and depth and are an effective way to gather broad input.

When you engage people to join your team, ask them to identify others for inclusion in such a virtual team for this extended review.

Invite participants

Many people close to a major change will have opinions, ideas, and concerns about how things should be handled. Engaging people to participate in a team that will help define strategy and decision-making may be an easy sell. But some of those whose input you need will be too busy or otherwise reluctant to devote the extra time to yet another project.

Where change isn't going well, some people will want to stay outside and resist the process. Challenge them to use their insights about the problem to develop solutions. Emphasize to potential team members the strategic importance of their participation.

Here are some tactics for encouraging participation:

- Be direct in stating that you'd rather have their input than work without it.
- Check with the individual's manager: "I'd love her to be involved but don't want to add to her workload—how can we manage it?"

---

9. A virtual team is a group that may be widely dispersed geographically and that rarely or never meets face-to-face. Instead they communicate by phone, e-mail, or Web-based resources.

- Plan the team's work in a way that accommodates the schedules of the people you most want to engage (e.g., location, duration, method—phone conferences when possible).
- Be flexible about permitting others to stand in from time to time for a key individual, provided they can bring the needed input and guidance.
- Offer resources or support to address competing demands or priorities; work with other initiatives and teams to put conflicting projects on hold.
- Use some people as reviewers rather than trying to engage them in primary planning or in a data-collection role.
- Be clear about your commitment to making the process tightly managed and time-efficient; follow up by ensuring that meetings are on schedule, focused, and productive.
- Emphasize the opportunity to be involved in an important task with an influence on the organization's success.

Bring the team together

In an initial meeting (live or electronic, depending on geographic dispersal, time, and resources), clarify the purpose of the project and roles of the team members. Starting with a discussion of the nature and status of the change will get everyone on the same page.

Part of this process will be determining the scope and scale of the team's work. This scope may be as modest as a brainstorming session with the current team to anticipate and document the major issues, or as broad as a large-scale assessment effort involving interviews, a survey, or other data-collection methods.

> **Get started with an agenda template**
> See Resource 2.2 (page 49) for a more detailed agenda you can modify to meet your needs.

Below is a suggested outline of agenda items for the tasks you'll work on as a team; other related tasks can be assigned to individuals. Use this as a starting point and modify it to meet your own needs.

- *Provide a welcome and overview:* Introduce the goals and key steps.
- *Update the team and discuss status:* Provide an overview of the initiative, and report on progress to date.

- *Review and refine (or develop) the plan:* Build the plan as needed; create a sense of ownership to ensure that the team will support it.
- *Define the primary issues:* Develop a preliminary list of the issues that led to this meeting, identifying factors indicating that change is off track or needs to be reinforced.
- *Determine next steps, responsibilities, and timing:* Map out a plan for assessment and correction, including who will do what and when.
- *Plan communication about the team's work:* Determine how and what to communicate about the work of the team; consider using a blog or other intranet resource to share ideas and information in real time.

If you're working on your own, in a smaller organization or on a local change, you can use the steps outlined above and perhaps enlist a small virtual review team of people involved in the change. Use this group to review your analysis, and to develop and confirm action steps in your plan.

PHASE 2: IDENTIFY AND DOCUMENT THE ISSUES

In local or small-scale changes, input may be gathered by having one or more meetings with people deeply and directly involved with the changes. In large-scale changes, it may be necessary and appropriate to conduct wider-ranging data collection to fully understand the issues, obstacles, and business impacts.

In either case, the first step is to draw on immediately accessible resources and information to summarize the issues and other factors that led to the need to refocus the change effort.

Following are suggested questions to guide the team in understanding and assessing the status of the change initiative. These are based on the seven core factors for managing change outlined on page 12.

The responses to these questions can provide a useful picture of how the change is going and where major issues lie.

Questions to assess the progress of change

For readers with limited time, Chapter 7 (page 207) provides a summary of the seven core factors, together with illustrative tactics for strengthening the process or for taking corrective action.

Clarity
- Are the purpose, direction, and approach of the change clearly defined and documented?
- Are these understood and accepted by key stakeholder groups?

Engagement
- Have stakeholders, especially those with major influence on the outcome, been involved significantly in the process?
- If so, has their input been acknowledged and applied?

Resources
- Are the needed resources (e.g., financial, human, other) in place to enable the change?
- Is there a strong and effective team in place to lead and guide the implementation of the change?

Alignment
- Do key systems and processes (e.g., rewards, information, accounting, training) support the change?
- Have needed changes to these systems and processes been developed and implemented?

Leadership
- Are leaders at all levels aware of, involved in, and committed to the change?
- Do leaders consistently follow up on issues, provide guidance and support, and proactively manage the process?

Communication
- Is clear, timely, and complete information available to the key audiences and stakeholders?
- Do these groups have access to additional information, answers to their questions, and a way of providing input and feedback?

Tracking
- Are systems in place to assess progress, including the financial and human impact of the change?
- Are adjustments being made as necessary?

Interpreting the data

If change is off track, it's likely that many responses to these questions will be negative. But they offer an immediate informal diagnosis of what might have contributed to the issues, and where solutions might lie.

To enable study of the issues and to develop tactics for action, you should look closely at negative responses to the questions above. Document known issues and obstacles that led to that assessment. Depending on timing and resources, these areas can offer direction for additional study. This might call for working with the stakeholders concerned, including employees, customers, suppliers, and others.

You might engage stakeholders in work teams or committees to clarify the issues and to develop solutions. This kind of involvement builds ownership—and can generate highly effective solutions.

To redirect change, you need current data about the organizational climate, and about the questions, concerns, and ideas of stakeholders who are dissatisfied.[10] This data can be a primary driver for planning. The issues and questions you uncover in the assessment process will determine the activities, including communication, process support, and training, that form your tactics for redirection.

PHASE 3: GATHER INPUT FROM STAKEHOLDERS

Stakeholders include those most involved in the change process, most affected by the outcome, and/or most able to influence the result. Collect input from these individuals and groups on results, issues, questions, and ideas for change. You need a complete picture of the status of the change effort and key issues that need to be resolved.

> **Use a checklist to identify stakeholders**
> Resource 2.3 (page 50) provides questions to help you select groups or individuals to include in your assessment.

Following are some of the major categories of stakeholders. If you'll be conducting an assessment, you'll need to decide which groups or individuals to include. You may engage only a few of these in the end, but identifying all significant stakeholders is an important step as you develop implementation plans.

---

10. Organizational climate describes the current status of employee attitudes, beliefs and expectations. It may change quite rapidly based on circumstances. By contrast, organizational culture is the totality of experience, traditions, beliefs, and norms. Culture can be an asset or liability, and is generally slow—and sometimes difficult—to change.

Primary stakeholder groups

Beyond the core stakeholders (employees, customers, shareholders, and other investors) there are several other groups with a stake in the outcome, or who are able to significantly influence it. It may take relatively little effort to identify these people and plan a process to inform and engage them. Yet the cost of failing to do so can be substantial if those concerned want or need to be involved in the process.

Core stakeholders
- Employees
- Customers
- Shareholders and other investors

Subgroups with significant involvement and major influence on the outcome
- Managers, supervisors, and team leaders
- Executive leadership (i.e., the individual or group leading or sponsoring the change)
- HR, IT, or other internal staff assisting the change effort
- Labor unions

Individuals or subgroups positively affected
- Employees with increases in salary, career opportunities, and/or job security
- Managers and employees with increased job responsibilities

Individuals or subgroups for whom the impact is undetermined
- People with increased responsibilities[11]
- IT specialists (e.g., those leading the integration of two merging organizations' computer systems)
- The HR specialist community
- Employees who remain after downsizing[12]

---

11. People in this group will probably be seen as gaining from the change, though they may not necessarily perceive themselves as "winners." The increase in work may not be welcomed, especially if it's not rewarded by a pay raise or promotion.

12. This group may experience or perceive increased workload without associated rewards or opportunities.

Individuals or subgroups negatively affected
- Employees who will lose their jobs or be forced to relocate
- Employees who will lose responsibilities, status, or pay

Other external stakeholders
- Board members
- Suppliers
- Business partners
- Government (e.g., regulators, state and local officials)
- Competitors
- Communities that may be affected economically or emotionally
- Families of employees
- Media (e.g., newspapers, trade publications; local TV and radio)
- Industry and professional associations

The role of HR

An important and often-overlooked group is the HR specialist community: HR professionals throughout the organization. This group typically plays a leading role in planning and executing change. HR staff may be closely involved with affected employees, providing counseling, coordinating training and job placement, handling administrative support, and supporting relocation efforts.

At the same time, they are likely to have issues and needs of their own, including concerns over their ability to perform expected tasks, their ongoing role, and their job security. Engaging HR specialists in the change process can provide invaluable data to guide communication and training efforts and ensure that this group is ready to handle the task.

Characteristics of effective progress assessment

Here are some of the keys to a successful progress assessment.

Prepare a core set of questions

Be consistent about what you ask. Develop a planned set of questions to ensure that you stay on track and cover all the key topics.

Consider the audience
Your assessment should include individuals who represent important stakeholder groups affected by the change. Prioritize the groups, perhaps based on the extent of their involvement.

Explore depth as well as breadth
Engage people at all levels, including those in a variety of functions and geographies. A diverse audience can provide a wide range of perspectives and ideas that can guide your planning.

Involve people close to the issues
People working directly with customers (e.g., in sales and technical support) may be at least as well-informed about how a change influences customer relationships as are the managers of those groups. Look to these people for candid feedback on what customers think—or are likely to think—about the change.

Expect, accept, and learn from negative opinions
If the data-collection effort is driven by a change initiative that's off track, you will certainly encounter strong criticism of the approach, its purpose, those leading it, and an array of other aspects. You need to value this criticism as data guiding development of new tactics.

Look for ideas
Make every effort to divert negative energy into a commitment to come up with ideas for getting back on track. Those involved in change, including those resisting it, usually have ideas about how it could be "done better." Many ideas will be useful and some may hold the key to success.

A useful by-product of this kind of data-collection effort is an array of Frequently Asked Questions (FAQs) encountered during the assessment. When organized into topics, with carefully prepared (but brief) responses, an FAQ guide is a useful resource for managers and others. See Chapter 6 on page 165 for more about developing FAQ guides.

Approaches to data gathering
A variety of approaches to gathering stakeholder information is available, ranging from fast and informal methods to lengthier, more elaborate, and more structured ones.

The amount and type of data you've already collected will help drive your approach for conducting the assessments. Some information will be available by monitoring ongoing communication in the organization (e.g., blog discussion threads can provide useful ideas and insight about issues and concerns). If your team has developed a significant amount of data based on its own experience and knowledge of the stakeholders, you might be able to gather the remaining input through informal e-mails or phone calls. But in larger-scale change, you will want to conduct more formal assessment using methods such as interviews, focus groups or online surveys. And social media are increasingly providing a very rich source of information and ideas within organizations.

The approach you take will also depend on your available resources and time. Here are some methods for conducting direct assessments.

Internal assessment

You can conduct assessments quickly and informally among the change team (and other internal groups) without formal "external" data collection. This approach is most effective if the team includes representatives from the major stakeholder groups.

Informal inquiry

This can be an effective approach in small-scale and/or local change. You can leverage routine ongoing interactions with members of various stakeholder groups to gather data. These interactions might include existing meetings, hallway discussions, and other interactions.

A concise set of standard questions that you and your team members ask at every opportunity will rapidly build up a significant and useful array of data.[13]

Social media

You can use social media passively—monitor blog responses, postings through Twitter, Yammer or other services, Facebook exchanges, and other data sources. Or you can create discussions and ask questions. With either approach, you can gain access to active, current, and relevant ideas and information.

---

13. See Resource 2.6 (page 55) for a list of possible questions.

As with any other data-collection method, you need to be aware of limitations—including the self-selection of contributors. But these methodologies certainly enable you to be aware of issues, concerns, and questions that you might not otherwise uncover.

E-mail-based assessments

E-mail-based assessments enable you to reach a broader sample and can provide solid data including useful qualitative input (ideas, opinions, and questions). The approach can be formal (include specific questions) or informal (ask one or two broad questions about the change). An active and well-followed blog can also generate input and ideas.

Small-group interviews

A direct Q&A approach is often conducted with workgroups. This works well when you have limited time and want to build involvement among key contributors. For example, in preparing for a change in sales information systems, you could bring together sales and customer service reps, marketing managers, and HR specialists who support these groups.[14]

Focus groups

Facilitated group discussions can be very useful for identifying unanticipated obstacles and quickly generating detailed feedback across a range of issues. Sharing findings and returning for follow-up discussions can also build participation in the change process.

You'll need to define group size, meeting location, time and duration, and other logistics.[15] Also decide who will facilitate the discussions, take notes, and manage follow-up.

Surveys (online or written)

You can administer a simple questionnaire in meetings or via e-mail, or you can use an online survey tool. This approach can provide quantitative data as well as qualitative input. If your organization doesn't have

---

14. You can also conduct small-group research through managers. Supply them with a suggested approach and set of questions, and ask them to meet with their teams to explore the issues. You achieve several goals: the data is collected; managers are involved in the process; team members contribute their ideas; workgroups meet to talk about change.

15. See Chapter 4 (starting on page 95) for more details about focus groups and resources for planning and conducting them.

online survey resources, you can find many available on the Internet. Several provide no- or low-cost packages: see Resource 2.7 (page 56).

Discussion guides and other tools

Whatever your approach to data collection, you will need to prepare a discussion guide or questionnaire. Even if your approach is an informal one, you need to be entirely clear about the three or four key questions you want to raise. Prepare for organized note-taking, either during the discussion or compiled later. Include the major questions and add space for responses, issues, ideas, and memorable observations.

You should also draft a concise introduction that sets the scene about the change and the assessment process. For example:

- Outline the context and purpose. State the goal of your assessment and emphasize the value that of feedback and input in contributing to a successful change.
- Clarify what you hope to accomplish. Emphasize that you need people to be candid about their perceptions and ideas, and that all feedback is welcome.
- Summarize the follow-up steps. Inform participants about what happens next, and how they'll be involved.

Perhaps the most commonly used question format provides four or five response options on a scale. Advocates of a four-part scale (strongly agree, agree, disagree, strongly disagree) believe that the structure forces respondents to take a position on each issue. By contrast, a five-part scale adds a "neutral/no opinion" option. The latter has the advantage that it allows for a response when the respondent is genuinely right in the middle (or genuinely undecided).

There is little evidence that four-part scales succeed in raising response rates: people who don't like the choices simply ignore the question. Accordingly, the resources and examples in this book use a five-part scale.

Multiple-choice scales (sometimes with as many as 10 options) are also used widely. These seem to be more suitable for consumer research with very large numbers of respondents. For an assessment of a group, team, or organization's readiness to deal with change, and where the person handling analysis and reporting may not be a trained researcher, a simpler scale will generally suffice.

Guidelines for survey design

If your organization has online survey capabilities, then you may want to use those. The survey process will be familiar to participants, and you may have support in development and deployment. If that option isn't available, look for a tool that offers at least these features:

- *Introduction page or statement:* Welcome respondents, explain the purpose of the survey, and describe how feedback will be used.
- *Navigation:* Be sure users can easily navigate forward and backward. They may want to refer to previous questions or return to ones they skipped.
- *Open-ended questions:* Provide a place for respondents to add their own comments and ideas. Make sure these will be automatically listed in the report—this is a significant advantage over having to manually copy and paste when compiling write-ins.
- *Useful reporting formats:* Test the format of reports by completing two or three questionnaires (ideally, have team members or others complete them and give you feedback on the process), then generate a draft report.
- *User-friendly tools:* Most online survey Web sites offer standard questionnaires that you can adapt, inserting your own questions in their format. These can work well, but you may prefer to design your own.

You can randomly select participants from your defined stakeholder groups, or ask managers from those groups to nominate people. Your approach may be influenced by work schedules and locations. Be sure that you can get adequate representation from each stakeholder group.

Approaching participants

Whether you approach employees directly or through a manager, provide a clear and concise explanation of the assessment and why participation is important.

Explain that your goal is to identify people who are representative of a group that will be affected by the change. Confirm that feedback will be confidential. Depending on the scale of the assessment effort, you may want to let nonparticipants know about the process and the reason their colleagues are attending meetings. Here are some considerations as you recruit:

- Does each group feel adequately represented? Make sure you have a participant to represent each key area or function.
- If people are reluctant to participate, is it because of schedule conflicts, or are there other reasons? Find out why and work to address the issues.
- Have any of the participants provided input for past changes? If so, do they feel satisfied about how their input was used, or frustrated that their feedback was ignored or did not influence decisions? If the latter, develop ways this time to ensure that their input is addressed directly.
- Are there important stakeholders who feel their opinions are rarely or never sought? If so, invite them to take part.

Send a reminder
It's helpful to send a reminder e-mail the day before a scheduled meeting. Remind participants of the purpose, location, time, and duration of the meeting.

Conducting assessments

Your primary goal for conducting an assessment is to obtain useful information about how key stakeholders will be affected by the change. Secondary goals may include initiating a process in which people are involved in the change and are able to contribute ideas and information.

As in any organizational assessment effort, you should also be committed to making the process a positive one for those involved. You want participants to feel that their ideas and opinions have been respectfully heard and will be applied appropriately. Following is a summary of steps for planning and conducting an assessment meeting:[16]

- Define the target group and selection method.
- Establish meeting location(s) and resources.
- Set meeting times and duration.
- Select and brief the meeting facilitators.

16. See Resource 2.5 (page 53) for a more detailed version of this logistics checklist.

- Invite participants and communicate with others as needed.
- Draft discussion materials.
- Prepare for note-taking and recording.
- Define your approach for verifying your findings.
- Determine the use for the information you gather.

Direct assessment enables you to engage a broad cross section of the organization. To get the most out of your meetings, develop a set of core questions. For example:

- What do people expect of the change?
- What will they need to make a successful transition?
- How has the change affected their work processes and goals?
- How can they (or how do they want to) influence and contribute to the change process?
- What obstacles or challenges exist? What's the best way to address them?

For those affected by the change, you can often address initial concerns and questions with straightforward and clearly-stated information. A robust change-summary document communicates the nature of the change, why it's happening, who will be involved, the key benefits, and how implementation will be handled.[17] It can be helpful to distribute this summary in advance of your meetings to ensure that stakeholders already have some insight about the change when you meet.

Summarize and verify feedback

After each meeting, draft a brief summary that highlights key points from the discussion, and verify the content with participants. This review loop is easy to execute via e-mail. Make it clear that additional feedback is welcome and that participants should provide corrections and clarifications as needed.

You will receive only a few comments or additions if your notes accurately reflect the tone and content of the meeting. However, this step demonstrates that the process is thoughtful, complete, and accurate.

---

17. See Chapter 3 (starting on page 67) for more information and resources on building a summary document for driving change.

When you send a summary, the accompanying cover letter (e-mail) should include a thank you for participation and a brief explanation of how feedback will used.

For example: "Thank you for attending the meeting. Your input will be included in a report used by the change team to improve planning. Your contribution will help ensure a successful transition."

Build confidence in the process
Ask participants to review meeting summaries. You will verify and strengthen your findings and communicate your intention to take feedback seriously.

PHASE 4: DEVELOP TACTICS AND TAKE ACTION

You now need to analyze the data you've collected, and use the results as you address the challenges and build on opportunities to keep the change on track—or restart it.

At the least, your stakeholder assessment is likely to provide a database of high-priority questions that need to be answered. You can then develop an FAQ document.

More broadly, your analysis is likely to yield a rich source of data on issues, opportunities, questions, and development needs. Topics may include customer education, employee training, leadership selection, and handling of job losses. Each issue can trigger the planning of a tactical response. Many successful change plans have been built by identifying stakeholder concerns and then systematically developing tactics and processes to address them.

Here are some recurrent findings in change research:

- *Change-readiness:* People often have concerns about their own readiness to adapt to change, and perhaps that of others. These concerns may focus on the ability to operate within a new sales environment, or to learn computer skills required by a new system, or to move into a new technical or management role. Responses may include training, guidance, and greater clarity about new roles.
- *Involvement:* Lack of employee involvement or consultation creates concern and frustration. The stakeholder assessment itself demonstrates a commitment to a higher level of involvement and consultation. Develop opportunities for people to contribute to and remain invested in making the change work.

- *Communication:* Employees directly affected by change almost invariably express a strong need for timely and accurate information. Building clear and efficient communication will be a high priority among the list of tactics.
- *Personal security:* Uncertainty about the personal impact ("What's going to happen to me?") may dominate some of the discussions. Appropriate ways of responding to those concerns need to be cited or developed—for example, through briefing and planning meetings led by managers or HR reps.

During the assessment, you may find people who want to directly participate in the management of the change, or who can contribute resources and ideas. Be sure to follow up and, where possible, engage these people in the process. This encourages participants to become more invested in the success of the change initiative and the organization as a whole. If you already have all the participants you need, you can still enlist interested individuals on a virtual review team.

Share your work with leaders of the organization and the change effort. Ensure that you have support for the tactics proposed, and resources available to implement them. After fine-tuning based on feedback, you can move forward to refocus plans an actions supporting the change.

The tactics and actions that are needed will be defined—or at least guided—by stakeholder assessment and other analyses. They may cover the full range of core factors. Examples of tactics and actions follow, and more are included in Chapter 7 (page 207).

Examples of tactics for driving or realigning change
Organized under the seven core factors, the examples that follow describe tactics that might be deployed in maintaining progress toward change, or regaining traction where the process is slipping. See also Resource 2.11 (page 60) for tactics to avoid common pitfalls.

Clarity
- Develop and distribute a summary document to serve as a core reference on the purpose and process of change.

- Develop a brief elevator pitch for managers—what's changing, and how it'll be done. [18]
- Provide managers with talking points on key questions.

In many change initiatives, the context, nature, and purpose of the change are not clearly spelled out for those involved and affected.

A clear summary document is an invaluable resource. It can refocus change and provide key stakeholders with source material, tools for communicating with others, and guidance on how to provide support.

Engagement

- Provide managers with guidance and tools to assist them to work with their teams to discuss the change and plan action.
- Ensure that senior leaders are visible and involved.
- Involve employees in planning and implementing change.
- Identify key stakeholders and conduct an assessment of their issues, questions, and ideas.

The process of studying the issues may build engagement. In addition, a candid discussion of issues and challenges can provide reassurance and reduce levels of concern even before a clear strategy for improvement has been developed.

Perhaps the key factor in engagement is the extent to which managers connect with, listen to, guide, and support their people. Prepare and support managers to fulfill this role by communicating and actively leading through the change process.

Resources

- Acknowledge the additional workload created by change efforts.
- Engage additional resources as needed (e.g., contractors).
- Facilitate adjustment of priorities to accommodate change.

Many change efforts fail because the needed resources (e.g., financial, human, equipment) aren't in place. Significant time and effort is needed to put a change into effect—developing new systems or struc-

---

18. You see an employee in an elevator or hallway, and she asks you about the change: "What's going on? Why are we doing this?" Your elevator pitch should answer these questions clearly, concisely, and positively—in 60 seconds or less.

tures, for example; or training those involved; or selecting people for key positions. But amid ongoing work demands, the added tasks may take second place and be poorly executed or even ignored.

A challenge for leaders is to recognize that some needed projects may have to be deferred if the change is to move forward effectively.

Alignment
- Assess key processes to ensure that they support the change.
- Add training and development programs as needed.
- Review and adjust communication processes and programs, and share information about the change to support alignment.

Alignment involves ensuring that business systems and processes collaborate in moving change ahead—or, at least, don't resist it.

Support systems need to be refocused to reinforce changes in, for example, the nature of the work, the structure of the organization, or business processes. It may be necessary to realign reward systems, communication, training programs, IT systems, and other processes.

Leadership
- Engage leaders through team activities.
- Address the concerns leaders may have about their role and responsibilities during and after the change process.
- Encourage leaders to promote behaviors and actions that will support the change.

A frequent complaint from those affected by change (but who are not leading it) is that they are being urged to behave in different ways while leaders seem to continue in former patterns of behavior. Examples include promoting open communication, respecting and addressing work-life challenges, and focusing on customers. A challenge for leaders is to ensure that those driving the change are aware of behavioral expectations and committed to fulfilling them.

Communication
- Include change-related information in existing media—and/or develop new processes to convey information (e.g., an intranet site focused on the change).

- Emphasize listening through formal and informal surveys, routine meetings and discussions, ongoing manager-employee conversations, and social media.
- Continually update and revise resources (e.g., FAQ guides, change-summary document, guides for managers).

Communication problems are often cited as a primary source of issues and delays in change, yet they can often be readily addressed. Communication needs to be managed as an ongoing two-way process rather than a one-way supply of information.

The communication process is also as much about understanding issues and needs as it is about providing information to the people involved. Effective communication ensures that those leading change are aware of issues, questions, and concerns; and that responses are provided in a timely and accessible way.

Tracking
- Conduct periodic surveys of stakeholders and/or monitor social media for commentary and questions about change.
- Include progress updates in meetings on other topics.
- Document questions and issues and ensure that responses are developed and shared.
- Maintain a focus on monitoring and course correction.

Follow-up is often forgotten in the pressure of day-to-day business. If leaders assume that the change process has been successful, but fail to verify that conclusion, problems may develop further and even derail the change.

People involved in change expect and need support and follow-up. They need to be asked what's working and what's not; they also need to be assured that their hard work and commitment are getting results and that change is helping the organization achieve the desired results.

PHASE 5: ASSESS PROGRESS AND COURSE-CORRECT

Leaders may initiate change and assume progress. In practice, old habits die hard; changes that are hard to implement may not become embedded; new behaviors may not develop; old habits may return.

Leaders need to stay in touch to review, assess, and apply course corrections. Progress can be monitored by ongoing meetings, social media, hallway discussions, and other interactions, as well as by assessment of business outcomes.

Also seek input from stakeholders. Once a feedback loop has been established, it opens an opportunity for ongoing monitoring. For example, if you have brought together groups of employees for focus groups or other meetings, you can check in periodically with those groups. This can be done by e-mail or in conference calls, both of which are less time-intensive than initial assessment meetings.

A quick follow-up inquiry ("How's it going? What's working? What's not? What should we do differently?") can yield useful data to help you understand what's happening, and to guide development of corrective action. Blogs maintained by leaders can stimulate constructive and informative discussion and idea-development.

Change rarely proceeds as planned and on course, without issues— foreseen or unforeseen—arising. Adjustments and corrections will almost invariably be needed. They may range from minor tuning (e.g., clarifying or extending responses to some of the questions in the FAQ guide) to major redirection (e.g., implementing new training programs to help employees acquire needed skills).

Materials used to educate, train, and communicate need to be revised periodically in light of additional questions and issues, and based on experience (positive and negative). Distributing revised versions provides a good opportunity for continuing to check in with key individuals and groups, and for evaluating status and progress.

A recurring theme that emerges in assessments of change efforts is, "We're making time to fix the problems; next time let's get it right the first time around."

RESOURCE 2.1: TEMPLATE FOR PROGRESS ASSESSMENT

This resource can assist in a rapid assessment of the status of a change initiative. Adapt it to meet your own needs. The assessment can be conducted informally (e.g., at meetings), via internal survey tools, or through a Web-based research site. Focus initial attention on factors that yield a 3 or 4. Response key: 1 = to a great extent; 2 = to some extent; 3 = not very much; 4 = not at all.

Core factor	Questions	1	2	3	4
Clarity	Are the purpose, direction, and approach to implementing change defined and documented clearly?				
	Are these understood and accepted by key stakeholder groups?				
Engagement	Have individuals and groups who can influence the outcome been involved in the process?				
	If so, have their input and ideas been acknowledged and applied?				
Resources	Are the needed resources (e.g., financial, human, technical) in place?				
	Is there a strong and effective team ready to lead and guide the change?				
Alignment	Do systems and processes (e.g., rewards, information, accounting, training) support the change?				
	Have changes to these systems and processes been developed and implemented?				
Leadership	Are leaders at all levels involved in and committed to the change?				
	Do leaders follow up on issues, provide guidance and support, and proactively manage the process?				
Communication	Is clear, timely, and complete information available to key audiences and stakeholders?				
	Do these groups have access to information, and a way of providing input and feedback?				
Tracking	Are systems in place to assess progress, and to identify issues that need to be addressed?				
	Are adjustments being made as necessary, and is information continuing to flow?				

RESOURCE 2.2: AGENDA FOR INITIAL TEAM MEETING
Build your own agenda to establish ground rules, agree on a process, and begin work.

Provide a welcome and overview
- Launch the process by introducing purpose, goals, and steps.
- Ask team members to briefly introduce themselves and outline their perspective on the change.
- Define the extent of team members' commitment to the project.

Update the team and discuss status
- Offer a brief overview of the change and its progress.
- Seek comments from team members.
- Use questions and discussion to get everyone on the same page about goals and issues.

Review and refine (or develop) the plan
- Discuss and refine the change plan as needed.
- Define the primary issues and concerns that led to the meeting.
- Document questions already raised about the change.
- Begin to allocate responsibilities.

Define needed assessment
- Determine assessment needs, including gathering opinions from stakeholders, benchmarking, and best-practice research.
- Discuss assessment approaches, such as interviews, social media, e-mail enquiry or focus groups.

Determine next steps, responsibilities, and schedule
- Map out the next steps, balancing the need for additional information with time and resource constraints.
- Identify needed resources and the process for acquiring them.
- Allocate responsibilities and establish a timeline; establish schedule, location, and other details for future meetings.

Plan communication
- Determine how and what to communicate to the team members' workgroups.
- Agree on a briefing process for leaders not on the team.

RESOURCE 2.3: CHECKLIST FOR IDENTIFYING STAKEHOLDERS

This checklist guides the identification of stakeholders affected by the change initiative, and organizes them into categories based on the extent of their involvement. Identifying all significant stakeholders is an important effort as you develop implementation plans, even if you engage with only a few of these groups.

Category	Stakeholders
Core stakeholders	Employees
	Customers
	Shareholders and other investors
Subgroups with significant involvement and major influence on the outcome	Managers, supervisors, and team leaders
	Executive leadership (i.e., the group sponsoring the change)
	HR, IT, or other staff assisting the change effort
	Labor unions
Individuals and subgroups affected by the change	*Individuals or subgroups positively affected*
	Employees with increases in salary, career opportunities, and/or job security
	Managers and employees with increased responsibilities in the new structure
	Individuals or groups for whom the impact is undetermined
	Specialists (e.g., IT, HR) involved in some aspects of the change
	Employees who remain after downsizing
	The HR community
	Individuals or subgroups negatively affected
	Employees who will lose their jobs or need to relocate
Other external stakeholders	Board members
	Suppliers
	Business partners
	Government (e.g., regulators, state and local officials)
	Competitors
	Communities that may be affected
	Families of employees
	Media (e.g., local, national, and trade publications and websites; radio and TV)
	Industry and professional associations

RESOURCE 2.4: ASSESSMENT METHODS

This resource provides an overview of assessment approaches. You need to gather feedback in a way that's straightforward, fast, and nondisruptive. Approaches can be informal (e.g., a brief discussion about the change in the course of day-to-day business) or highly structured (e.g., an online survey of a large group of stakeholders). The chosen approach will depend on time constraints, available resources, the culture of the organization, and the nature of the issues.

Face-to-face conversation

You can learn a lot by asking people questions in the course of everyday work, whether in person, by phone, by e-mail, at lunch, or during breaks in meetings:

- "How's it going with the changes?"
- "Any issues or problems we should know about?"
- "What's working, and what isn't? How can we assist?"

This method may not achieve comprehensive coverage of the right stakeholders. The data and insights that you gather may not be complete, consistent, or convincing to leadership. A few people with strong opinions could influence your assessment. But you can learn a great deal in a short time. This is often the first step in working toward a more formal effort.

E-mail survey

Gather information via email from people involved in the change. Provide some structure (e.g., a few core questions) to facilitate the assessment, and some guidance on the depth of response you're seeking ("Provide no more than a sentence or two for each response …").

You will likely gather some useful feedback, but the stronger the response, the greater the task of compiling and summarizing the data. There could be a great deal of input in a variety of formats.

Social media

Twitter, Yammer, Facebook, and many other systems can be a rich source of information and ideas about what people are experiencing and thinking. Explore ways to use these, matching the medium to the stakeholder group.

RESOURCE 2.4 [CONTINUED]

Online survey

An online survey is an effective way to gather a large volume of feedback quickly and easily. Most survey tools allow you to design your questions in a variety of formats (e.g., multiple-choice, ranking, open-ended), and the tools compile the results for you. One advantage of more formal surveys is that they enable a degree of automation in tabulating results. Data obtained from surveys can be compelling, including quantitative assessments of progress as well as commentary about issues.

Manager-facilitated assessment

Provide questions to managers and other leaders and ask them to engage their teams to gather feedback. They might introduce the topic at team meetings and lead discussion of issues and needs.

This approach encourages managers to think about how the change has been proceeding. It forces them to reflect on their role in leading the change. And it stimulates discussion about local operational issues—helping to drive the change process to the front line.

Consider meeting with managers to prepare them for these discussions, and equip them with a guide. Follow up to share feedback and discuss next steps. Once again, your interaction with managers, and their interactions with their teams, is an important part of enabling change.

Special meetings (interviews and focus groups)

If you need to conduct a more intensive assessment, you can organize and conduct informal meetings with employees, managers and others. You may want to conduct focus groups with stakeholders (see Chapter 4, starting on page 95). These are moderated discussions, typically lasting 60 to 90 minutes, in which a facilitator presents questions and guides the group through responses and discussion.

Composite approach

You might combine a number of the above methods for a more comprehensive assessment. Monitor blogs and other online forums; use informal discussions to assess the nature and scope of issues; distribute an online survey to reach a wider audience; and work with managers to engage their teams to discuss concerns and needed actions.

RESOURCE 2.5: ACTION ITEMS FOR MEETING PLANNING

This list provides guidance for planning meetings (one-to-one, small group, focus group, or other) with stakeholders.

Item	Decisions and action items
Target group and selection method	Define the target group (e.g., first-level supervisors in departments implementing the new system).
	Determine a selection method (e.g., random, nominations by managers).
	Define the sample and the group size.[19]
Meeting location and resources	Decide where to conduct the meetings and what facilities and supplies are needed (e.g., refreshments, flip charts).
	Choose a location that's convenient and comfortable for participants.
Meeting time and duration	Determine when to hold the meetings and how much time you need: meetings of 60 to 90 minutes are typical for group interviews and focus groups.
	Schedule at least 15 and preferably 30 minutes between meetings to allow for transitions between groups, give the facilitator a break, and allow time to refresh the room.
Facilitator	Decide who will facilitate the discussion. Your team may have people with the right skills and experience.
	Facilitators may also be found in HR, training, or organizational development groups; or consider hiring an external consultant.
Invitations and communication	Distribute invitations to participants.
	Communicate as needed (if appropriate, in advance) with supervisors whose employees will be involved.
	Explain the meeting's purpose and process, and also define the time commitment.

---

19. The sample specifies the number of participants and where they come from, defined by characteristics such as location, function, or role.

RESOURCE 2.5 [CONTINUED]

Factor	Issues and decisions
Discussion materials	Prepare a discussion guide and/or survey forms.
	Prior to the meeting, share the plan and the guide with those involved in the process; seek feedback and ideas for improvement.
	Test the content and approach on one or two people and make changes as needed.
Note-taking and recording	Decide how to record the input and who will manage that process. Your goal is capture an accurate account of stakeholder feedback.
	Consider scheduling two people to run each meeting: one to focus on facilitating the discussion; the other to take notes.
	Determine whether notes will be shared visibly with the group (e.g., via a flip chart).
Verification and follow-up	Determine who will prepare meeting summaries and manage verification and follow-up with participants.
	Decide who will prepare the report and manage the review with the extended team.
Logistics	Document logistical needs for meetings (e.g., rooms, resources, refreshments, equipment, facilitators) and assign responsibility.

RESOURCE 2.6: TEMPLATE FOR A DISCUSSION GUIDE

You can adapt this model, modifying or extending the questions to match the issues and needs of your organization. Inviting people to contribute ideas demonstrates the organization's interest in input and involvement. Also draw on the assessment questions listed on page 31.

Area	Core questions
Clarity of purpose: Determine how well people understand the reasons for change.	Do you clearly understand the purpose and nature of the change? What information is unclear or incomplete?
Reactions to process: Explore how people feel about the change and the way it's being managed; gauge levels of satisfaction or resistance.	In general, is the transition progressing smoothly for you and your team? Do you feel the transition is being managed well? How has the change affected your job and how you do it? Has your manager been keeping you informed and involved? Are you getting support for the challenges the change creates? Is your manager supporting your development? How could the transition be improved? What additional steps could your manager take to move the change forward more effectively?
Resource needs: Learn what people need in terms of staffing, support, training, and equipment.	Are you and your teams effectively managing any increased workload? Do you have resources (e.g., people, equipment, budget) to meet new demands? Are you (or your team) receiving needed support? Do you (or your team) have access to training or mentoring for developing skills? What is still needed? What are the obstacles to getting what you need?
Ideas and comments: Explore other suggestions and opinions about the change.	What obstacles or issues need to be addressed? What questions still need to be answered? Do you have any other opinions you would like to share, or ideas for how we might move the process forward more effectively?

RESOURCE 2.7: WEB-BASED SURVEY TOOLS

These online survey resources do not charge for small- or medium-scale surveys. Most allow you to create a questionnaire with a variety of question formats (multiple choice, rating bars, comments, rankings). You can invite participants either via e-mail sent from the Web site or via your own e-mail containing a link to the survey. You create an account to view compiled responses and edit your surveys. Some of the organizations listed also offer premium survey tools, which include advanced customization and allow you to survey large audiences.

Zoomerang www.zoomerang.com	A basic version of the tool is free: view responses for up to 10 days, and get results downloaded in spreadsheet format.
WebSurveyor's RSVME www.rsvme.com	Create e-mail surveys. The tool integrates with Microsoft Outlook, enabling you to conduct surveys within e-mail, and also summarizes responses for you.
Vovici www.vovici.com	Create comprehensive online surveys in a variety of formats.
SurveyMonkey www.surveymonkey.com	A basic subscription is free: the free surveys are limited to 10 questions and 100 responses.
FreeOnlineSurveys www.freeonlinesurveys.com	Create and edit online surveys using a variety of question formats. You can add images; skilled users can edit in HTML.

RESOURCE 2.8: TEMPLATE FOR AN E-MAIL SURVEY

For small-scale changes, you might conduct an informal survey by simply asking questions via e-mail. Although participants may find this approach more time-consuming than a check-the-box online survey, it can work well for gathering qualitative input from a small group. Here is suggested text for the e-mail.

Subject: Assessing progress with the change

We're gathering input to strengthen the change process by learning what's working well and what needs improvement.

Please keep your responses to the questions below quite brief—one or two sentences each. And while we certainly want to learn about problems and challenges, we're also eager to hear your ideas for how we can improve the process and ensure that the change succeeds.

Please respond as soon as you can but in any case by *[time]* on *[date]*. We'll share a summary with you, along with management's responses and plans. Meanwhile, don't hesitate to let me know if you have any immediate comments or questions about this process.

1. Do you clearly understand the purpose and goals of the change?

2. If not, what information is unclear or incomplete?

3. Do you think the transition process has been effective?

4. If not, how could it be improved?

5. Have you had appropriate support, guidance, resources, and training?

6. If not, what do you need?

7. What questions or issues have not been answered or addressed?

8. Do you have any other ideas or opinions you would like to share about ways we can keep the process moving forward effectively?

Many thanks for your time and feedback!

RESOURCE 2.9: TEMPLATE FOR ASSESSMENT QUESTIONNAIRE

Keep surveys brief: 12 to 15 questions are reasonable, with fewer than half being open-ended. Try to limit surveys that are comments-only to 5 or 6 questions. A five-point scale is available from most survey providers but you can structure questions in other ways, including ranking and yes-or-no responses. The example below (with instructions to circle a response) can be used for an informal pen-and-pencil survey.[20] It can also be adapted for online use. Key: 1 = to a great extent; 2 = to some extent; 3 = neutral/ no opinion; 4 = not very much; 5 = not at all.

Do you understand the nature of the changes?	1	2	3	4	5
Do you understand the purpose?	1	2	3	4	5
Do you agree that the changes are needed?	1	2	3	4	5

What major obstacles need to be overcome?

What factors are working in favor of change?

Do you understand how the changes affect you?	1	2	3	4	5
Have you been able to contribute your ideas?	1	2	3	4	5
Have you been able to raise questions?	1	2	3	4	5
Do you feel ready to make the changes?	1	2	3	4	5
Are needed resources in place (e.g., training)?	1	2	3	4	5
Do you think that your manager is prepared?	1	2	3	4	5
Does your manager have needed resources?	1	2	3	4	5
Are you involved in decisions that affect you?	1	2	3	4	5

If you could make one change to the process, what would it be?

Please use this space for any further comments and ideas.

Many thanks for your help!

---

20. For example, the leader of a team meeting might ask participants to complete a questionnaire. This can be done quickly, will likely stimulate useful discussion, and provides results that can be quickly reviewed and summarized.

RESOURCE 2.10: SAMPLE E-MAIL FOR SURVEY DISTRIBUTION

Here is sample text you can use for an e-mail inviting people to respond to an online survey. Adapt the message to suit your needs by incorporating your own specific purpose and goals. This kind of assessment can effectively emphasize that those managing the change are open to opinions and ideas about progress and issues.

Subject: Progress check

We're *[number]* weeks into the *[name of change initiative]*, and *[individual or team]* is looking for feedback on how the process is going and what steps we can take to ensure we stay on track and move forward smoothly.

Our goal is to make sure that we're putting our resources and efforts in the right places. We've been gathering input on metrics and costs, but we're also very interested in feedback about the impact on people and teams who might need additional support.

As you're part of a group that's been deeply involved in the change, we would appreciate hearing your opinions and ideas about how things are going. We have developed a brief survey and would appreciate you taking a few minutes to answer some key questions about issues and needs that affect you and your team.

As well as the multiple-choice, there's an option to add your own comments on any issues related to the change. We welcome your opinions and ideas.

We're looking for your quick and candid assessment to help give us an up-to-date picture of our progress—and guide us on any tactics we need to put into action. We need everyone to complete the survey by *[time]* on *[date]*.

Here is the link: *[URL]*

We'll compile the responses and provide *[individual or group]* with a report outlining progress, issues, and needs. We will of course share a summary with those who participate in the survey.

We much appreciate your help and look forward to getting your input. If you have any immediate questions or comments, please let us know at *[e-mail]*.

RESOURCE 2.11: CHECKLIST ON AVOIDING THE PITFALLS

This resource provides examples of some of the pitfalls that abound in change initiatives, aligned with the relevant core factors for managing change.[21] Each pitfall is listed with suggested tactics for sustaining or reinforcing change. Identify the issues that your initiative is facing and consider some of the suggested tactics.

Pitfalls	Tactics
Core factor: Clarity	
The case for change is unrealistic or incomplete.	Build a robust, complete, and convincing case for change.
	Drive urgency (e.g., by defining a "burning platform"—a crisis that compels action; describing competitive successes; or discussing negative customer feedback).
	Study cultural support or obstacles (e.g., prior initiatives, patterns to repeat or avoid).
Core messages are buried in a mass of detailed strategic planning materials.	Create a short, clear, and useful summary as a reference for managers and other stakeholders.
	Develop a truly concise (one minute or less) summary for managers to adapt and use: an elevator pitch.
Basic elements of the case for change are not memorable or not readily understood.	Build a strong plan that can be clearly communicated.[22]
	Provide a compelling rationale: a coherent and understandable vision and plan.
	Emphasize brevity and clarity in all communication materials dealing with the change.
Managers do not consistently support the direction of change.	Work with managers (and other opinion leaders) to build commitment and support; involve them in planning and action.[23]

---

21. See page 12 for a review of the core factors in successful change management.
22. If you can't explain it, the plan is probably flawed. At best, it will be hard to sell.
23. Opinion leaders may be influential managers or leaders, but may also be rank-and-file employees who command respect through their behavior, achievements or character.

RESOURCE 2.11 [CONTINUED]

Pitfalls	Tactics
	Use key managers on a virtual review team to provide guidance as plans are developed. [24]
	Provide resources to help managers deal with change and resistance.
	Establish ongoing communication (e.g., a weekly conference call to review progress and issues).
There's a lack of clarity about roles, responsibilities, and authority.	Ensure that leaders (of the organization and/or the initiative) provide clear direction.
	Explicitly define roles and responsibilities.
Core factor: Engagement	
Leaders assume that they know what people think and don't test assumptions.	Identify those who may resist change, understand their issues, and plan responses.
	Gather information wherever and whenever possible, through informal and formal means; always ask, "How is this going? What could we do differently?"
	Involve skeptics: seek their ideas and encourage them to contribute to the process.
	Encourage leaders to meet with managers, employees, and others for briefings and discussions about the change; encourage two-way communication.
Key people or groups are not involved because of their current commitments and workload.	Identify formal and informal leaders; get buy-in to drive and influence the process.
	Dedicate the right resources to the change: not only the people with time available.
	Transfer workload from key people, engage additional resources, or defer projects, to enable energy and time to be focused on change management.
Questions and ideas are inadequately recorded, documented, and used.	Maintain a database of questions and issues.
	Use the database to build resources such as an FAQ guide, and to identify issues that need resolution.
	Build an online resource where people can ask questions and get answers.

---

24. A virtual team can work through e-mail, phone conferencing, or other remote methods. Members can be located in any geographic area or time zone, and the time commitment can be quite limited. Use of a virtual team is an effective way of engaging people across the organization and generating feedback and guidance.

RESOURCE 2.11 [CONTINUED]

Pitfalls	Tactics
Core factor: Resources	
The costs of change are not recognized or funded.	Include assessments of cost, time, and other resources in planning.
	Ensure that the organization's and the initiative's leaders recognize the costs, and approve and support the plan and its use of resources.
	Assess the financial impact of successful change and demonstrate the value of investing in a successful transition.
Leaders and other team members are assigned to tasks without assessment and management of their core workload.	Find ways to ensure that key people in leadership roles driving change are able to focus fully on that task without a high cost in lost focus on customer service or other key activities.
	Use temporary transfers, changes in planning priorities, temporary staff, and other strategies to manage the workload of key people and groups.
Training and/or other support processes aren't adequate to equip people for the change.	In research and discussion about the change, gather input from stakeholders on the training or support they need to be able to handle the change.
	Where new skills are needed, provide resources and processes (e.g., training, information, development) to help people build them.
Core factor: Alignment	
Plans for change are limited or incomplete	Gather information and build a plan that addresses the need for systems and processes to be adjusted where necessary to support the changes that are occurring.
	Examine and answer the key stakeholder question: "What's in it for me?"
Needed systems (e.g., rewards, information) are not in alignment.	Identify areas where support is needed and ensure that systems are managed and developed to provide that support.
	Ensure and monitor systems support (e.g., IT, rewards, assessment).
	Identify and address processes or provisions that are inconsistent with or resist the change (e.g., incentive pay systems that reward individual results in a situation where the focus is moving to teamwork).

RESOURCE 2.11 [CONTINUED]

Pitfalls	Tactics
Core factor: Leadership	
Leaders call for change from others without demonstrating the same commitment.	Build buy-in from leader-managers at all levels. Clearly define needed new behaviors, skills, and attributes (as well as structures and processes). Identify and describe actions that run counter to the model (e.g., not displaying needed teamwork or failing to communicate). Ensure that leaders understand the need for changed behavior, and adopt and demonstrate it themselves.
Leaders of change efforts are not consistently recognized and rewarded.	Provide recognition, reinforcement, and rewards. Guide senior leaders to ensure that those deserving support receive it.
Progress and setbacks aren't communicated; wins aren't celebrated.	Be open and direct about what the change achieves, and what it doesn't; define what's needed to keep it or get it on track. Give credit where it's due to those who make significant contributions to the process.
Senior leaders don't show consistent attitudes toward the need for change or their roles in making it happen.	Identify trusted and respected leaders and involve them in the process. Provide objective feedback if leaders' behavior is failing to support change. Engage other senior managers to model and encourage supportive leadership behavior.

RESOURCE 2.11 [CONTINUED]

Pitfalls	Tactics
Core factor: Communication	
One-way communication (e.g., e-mail) is used for complex changes.	Build a two-way communication process to ensure that adequate information is presented, questions are answered, and adequate opportunities are provided for discussion.
	Establish ongoing communication forums (e.g., town-hall meetings, manager conference calls, webinars, local team meetings).[25]
Communication methods are not audience-focused (e.g., messages aren't integrated into routine meetings).	Provide managers and others with templates and summaries to make it easy for them to build in discussion of the change.
	As needed, provide guidance and training on communication and meeting leadership.
Messaging about the change addresses only one side of the issue.	Acknowledge and discuss the negatives as well as the positives—those involved will do so in any case, and you want to be part of that discussion.
	Limit or acknowledge ambiguity (e.g., say what you do and don't know).
	Be clear about what will change and what won't.
	Be ready to engage in discussion about the change and its impact, even when direction or outcomes haven't yet been fully defined.
Leaders' focus is on issues of low concern to employees.	If one aspect of the change is likely to receive major attention from employees (e.g., effect on job security), you must address it fully and openly.
	By addressing the issue you will enable people to move on to think about their role and other issues.
Those involved have limited opportunity to discuss, challenge, and question the change process.	Use open dialog and communication; expose hidden agendas; communicate continually.
	Provide multiple opportunities for people to provide input and ask questions.
	Accept dissenting opinions; permit expression of negative viewpoints.

25. Webinars are Web-based seminars.

RESOURCE 2.11 [CONTINUED]

Pitfalls	Tactics
Core factor: Tracking	
The organization makes a premature assumption of success, then loses focus on the change.	Maintain version control;[26] update the map; adjust the process as needed.
	Follow up; provide feedback on progress; and close the loop.
	Create and celebrate early wins to build and maintain momentum.
Managers and others return to old ways of doing business.	Execute the plan; monitor and follow up; identify and resolve problems and issues.
	Stay committed to change; never assume that change will happen without effort, commitment, testing, and course correction.
No measurement systems are in place.	Establish clear goals and measures (e.g., managers trained, sales teams formed, customer briefings held, employee support assessed, customer satisfaction maintained).
	Measure outcomes through surveys and existing information systems; report results.
	Validate and check continually by inviting comments and assessment.
There is limited follow-up and assessment; issues go unrecognized and un-addressed.	Identify key issues and obstacles—matters that are given "must resolve" status.
	Foster flexibility and resilience with clarity, education, support, leadership, and resources.
	Document issues and concerns, and report regularly to senior leaders on solutions and approaches to addressing problems. When necessary, engage those leaders in developing and implementing solutions.

---

26. The meaning of (and need for) version control quickly becomes apparent when someone makes changes to a document and then receives detailed comments and edits on an earlier version of that document. If many people are providing input the process can become exceptionally time-consuming and complex. Microsoft Word has tools (including Track Changes) to manage this process, and online resources such as Google Docs also provide resources for document management and review. In summary, be clear about the review process and avoid making revisions before you have heard from those asked to contribute.

RESOURCE 2.12: TACTICS FOR A CHANGE-READY TEAM

Many organizations begin to focus on alignment, involvement, communication, strategic clarity, and other factors only when change is imminent—or in progress. But these attributes can't always be readily created: the process takes effort, time, and commitment. That's why it makes sense to start managing change before it happens. It makes sense to build a change-ready environment in which people seek, welcome, and adapt to change. This worksheet suggests a set of tactics. For each item, develop ideas and plans for working with your own team.

	Tactic
1	Lay the groundwork as far in advance as you can. Keep your team informed about possible developments and needed changes.
2	Look for early warnings on issues and obstacles. As you engage the team in discussion of plans, use "what if" questions to uncover potential obstacles.
3	Engage your team in planning for change. Challenge them to identify needed changes, to seek opportunities, and to develop implementation plans.
4	Share the workload. Recognize the demands of day-to-day operations; ensure that workloads are balanced and resources appropriately shared.
5	Recognize limitations on time and energy. Ask people what support they need (e.g., defer projects; reassign workload; share tasks; shift priorities).
6	Build satisfaction and a sense of achievement around change. Celebrate and reward success; don't punish failures—study them and learn from them.
7	Look for feedback at every opportunity. Ask people how they're doing, what they think, what ideas they have, and how you can help.
8	Be involved and accessible. Make sure everyone knows that you're available and that you welcome discussion and input—and be sure to respond.
9	Recognize strong performance. Provide feedback and public acknowledgement of how a certain effort or achievement made a difference.
10	Respect all input. Don't react badly to bad news, or you won't hear it the next time. Listen, assess, and plan to address the problem or concern.
11	Demonstrate values and behaviors you want your team to display. Be open, be customer-focused, build diverse teams, respect work-life balance, listen.[27]
12	Continually seek change and improvement. Beware of finding comfort in the status quo—never stop looking for ways to improve.

27. Modify as appropriate to align with your own leadership approach and values.

CHAPTER 3

Making the case for change

BUILDING AN EFFECTIVE SUMMARY DOCUMENT

Clarity is the first of the seven core factors in successful change. And while these factors form a framework rather than a linear process, clarity about strategy and direction might be considered a starting point for successful management of change.

To plan and execute a successful change effort, you need to be clear about purpose, direction, and approach. A highly effective method for achieving this clarity is development of a comprehensive summary document. This provides a clear and concise explanation of what's changing and why, how it will happen, and who will be involved. The document describes the context, purpose, and plans for change; and links the change to the broader needs of the business.

A focused and effective summary document—built around the business case—supports the change process in several ways:

- It supports consistent messaging and reduces the need to repeatedly develop new materials.
- It exercises a forcing function—early in the planning process—through which the organization verifies that the case for change is clear, complete, and appropriate.
- It ensures that the purpose, rationale, and process for the change are clearly defined and understood, and it develops a foundation for building trust in the process.
- It helps the organization communicate effectively and tell a compelling story about the change.

Overall, the document ensures clarity and provides the platform to support other factors, including communication and engagement.

This chapter provides guidance for creating a summary document for driving change. Tools and source materials, including a template for the document, are included in the resources beginning on page 80.

These resources can't cover every situation or need. In some cases you may be part of a large team; in other cases you may be working alone. In some cases you may have a rich source of material to draw on (strategic planning data, competitor analyses), and in others you may be doing your own assessment. Adapt the materials as needed.

CLARIFYING STRATEGIC INTENT

It's not uncommon for there to be no core strategic plan for change. Major changes are often conceived at a high level, perhaps by the CEO and a small team, and based on broad strategic purpose. The point of view considered is that of the shareholder, while the concerns of other stakeholders may be secondary or even overlooked.

The change initiators see the broad business landscape and decide that the change makes strategic sense, but often leave the execution and details to others. Bridging the gap between strategic concept and implemented reality presents many challenges. A strong summary document can address some of those.

The change addressed in the summary can be strategic and organization-wide (e.g., a merger) or tactical and local (e.g., reorganization of a sales team). It can be straightforward and executed quickly (e.g., new express-shipping arrangements) or complex and sustained (e.g., transfer of operations to a new manufacturing facility).

Every change process is different, but the task of developing a summary document will probably fall into one of these three broad categories—and very often into the first:

- The high-level decisions have been made but not clearly documented, and the process and plan are still undeveloped.
- The business case is clear, but the implementation plan is undeveloped or in the very early stages of development.
- The business case and implementation plan have already been clearly defined and documented.

The approaches and tools in this chapter can be adapted for each of these situations.

Case history: The value of a robust business case

A medical-equipment company was expanding fast by internal growth as well as through acquisitions. The announcement that manufacturing was to be consolidated into a single new Midwest plant (from several locations in the US and Mexico) raised questions and concerns across the organization.

Would people lose their jobs or have to relocate? How would expertise be retained and applied in the new plant? Was the change motivated by cost reduction? Had other approaches had been explored? What would be the impact on production cycles, product lines, and development teams?

A transition steering group had been established, with several teams working on issues including technology and processes, relocation logistics, financial planning, HR policies and issues, and communication. The group's role was to focus on the mechanics of executing the change.

To support transition planning, the communication team was asked to draft a concise planning document covering the rationale and the process for implementing the change.

The team found it hard to get started. The leader explained, "There's no real plan for us to summarize, at least not one that's been documented. The decision was made by the board based on a presentation from the CEO and the planning team. They talked about industry economics and financial implications.

"But they never addressed the human impact and how we would actually get this done. The transition group doesn't have the answers and information we need. And they're looking for this business case. We need to start from square one."

The team asked key executives for brief outlines of purpose, rationale, process, and key implementation steps. They then compiled a draft, working with peers from each major functional area. The draft summary was offered to the executives for review, input, and approval.

Along the way, many changes were made to the document. But the framework that the team developed jump-started planning, identified major issues to be addressed, and clarified priorities. It provided a useful starting point, and evolved into a key change-management tool.

When the final version reached the CEO, his comment was, "I wish I'd had this when we made the case to the board."

PROCESS FOR CREATING A SUMMARY DOCUMENT

An effective summary document is a powerful tool for building support for change among employees, customers, and other stakeholders. It's also a useful tool for ensuring that all who are involved in planning and implementation operate from a consistent source. Summarized below is a simple six-phase process for working with a team to develop and deploy a summary document. A detailed discussion of each phase follows.

Phase 1: Form a team

Build a team of people with the right experience, skills, and knowledge to offer input and guidance.

Phase 2: Develop or clarify the core message

Start by creating a shared understanding about the change, including its purpose, nature, and rationale: often referred to as the business case.

Phase 3: Define communication plans

The summary document should include an outline of how the change will be communicated to employees, customers, and other key audiences. If a plan is already in place, then this phase will focus more on summarizing the work that's been done.

Phase 4: Compile the summary document

Develop an initial draft document covering the change, its impact, and the communication process.

Phase 5: Engage others to build consensus

Share the draft summary with a broader audience in order to gather additional feedback, build alliances, and gain support for the change.

Phase 6: Deploy the document

Move from testing to application. Distribute the summary document or make it available online. Ensure that questions are addressed and that feedback is collected, assessed, and applied, so that the material continues to support and drive the change process.

Phase 1: Form a team

The primary purpose of this team is to develop a strong and accurate summary document by engaging key stakeholders and gathering input from multiple sources.

This may be just one of several teams working on the transition. Other teams might be looking at systems integration, marketing and sales, legal issues, employment and HR matters, training, stakeholder communication, and other issues. Team leaders may be part of a broad steering committee or transition team.

Enlist a strong writer
Be sure that you have someone on the team with excellent writing and editing skills.

In smaller organizations, or where less complex changes are in progress, your team may itself be the group guiding the overall process and working on all aspects of change management.

The business case will be stronger and less subject to challenge if key contributors have the opportunity to offer input and guidance on how the change is planned and how it gets communicated.

Whether the change is organization-wide or local, engage the most involved and informed people for your team—those who will be directly affected, able to influence the process, and/or those who have important knowledge about the circumstances of the change.

Resources for team formation
Resource 3.1 (page 80) provides a sample e-mail invitation that outlines team purpose, roles, and process.

Members of your team might include:

- The leader (and/or sponsor) of the change process
- Representatives from key stakeholder groups (especially those likely to be positively or negatively affected by the changes)
- One or two key managers whose operations will be affected
- Sales managers who can represent your customers' perspectives
- Specialists, such as HR staff, with experience and skills that will be helpful in managing change

You should also include one or more individuals with strong writing skills. They can take the lead in putting the document together and ensuring that it's consistent, clear, and concise.

Phase 2: Develop or clarify the core message

With the team in place, your primary goal is to concisely document the nature of the change and the business case that's driving it. You'll need to outline what the change is about, how it will work, and how it will be implemented and communicated.

The core message focuses on the "what" and "why" of the change. Giving people a roadmap builds support, participation, and commitment to a successful outcome. Start by developing messaging about the change itself and the business rationale behind it.

To launch your process, gather the team in a face-to-face meeting or phone conference. In addition to outlining the purpose and process for creating the summary document, this initial meeting gives everyone the chance to learn who's involved and how each person can contribute.

Focus on the impact and meaning of the change. When people face change, whether it is of their own choice (e.g., accepting a new job) or something forced on them (e.g., a reorganization or major new process), they generally want to know four things immediately:

- How will this affect me?
- Why are we doing this?
- Where can I get answers?
- What should I do next?

The questions about individual impact may not be answered in the early stages of a change. These questions may have to await detailed implementation planning and decisions about matters such as staffing, promotions, job losses, relocations, and role changes. But you can reduce the uncertainty by providing guidance on timing issues. For example:

> **Make a convincing case for change**
> Resource 3.3 (page 82) includes ideas and tactics for communicating the case for change.

- "No job losses will happen before the end of the year."
- "Open leadership positions will be listed on June 1."
- "Enrollment for systems training will start next week."
- "During the next six weeks, all reps will be involved in defining the new sales teams."

The sense of stability and control of those involved in major changes can be disturbed. Answering these questions may help restore that sense of control. When people clearly understand why something is happening, how it will affect them, and also how they might benefit, they feel reassured and motivated. Effective communication around these issues helps to advance a change effort successfully.

People will have business concerns as well. The summary should also address these common questions:

- *What's this all about?* Present the story behind the change and the facts about plans and process for execution.
- *What will be different?* A vision of the outcome or results of the change provides an effective response.
- *What's the value?* Outline the benefits and opportunities for employees, customers, and other affected stakeholders.
- *How will it affect our bottom line?* Discuss and describe the expected impact on the business.

Listen to objections and understand the sources and causes of resistance. Acknowledge stakeholder concerns and respond to them clearly and directly. If you ignore objections, they will most likely surface somewhere else where you may not have the opportunity to address them. You can avoid that by being well-prepared to communicate a solid case for change early in the process.

Be aware of history Look at your organization's track record on managing change. This can inform your approach to preparing a strong and compelling story, and building support to make the change work.

Also keep in mind that organizations have different patterns of response and agility around change. Some are change-ready and adapt easily; others are heavily invested in the status quo, unused to change, and likely to struggle with the process.

Trust develops when people see openness, directness, and honesty. Tell both sides of the story, including negatives and real or potential problems: your credibility will be strengthened. Most changes carry risks and costs (e.g., system changes that reduce customer service levels during the transition). If you address the issues directly, people can see that the issues are recognized and understood. They feel more prepared and maintain a sense of control over their work.

Phase 3: Define communication plans

With a clear message about the change and the business rationale, you can now define how the change will unfold, and build support. You will document (or develop) a high-level communication plan.

The core message focuses on the "what" and the "why." The plan should summarize the "how," "who," and "when." These are the highlights of logistics for rolling out the change. The plan will be strengthened as you test it and get feedback and gain insights from the people you engage during the process. It can also serve as the foundation for more detailed planning efforts.

If a formal change plan has already been fully documented, you can borrow from that plan to create this part of the summary document. If you're starting from scratch, the summary document can serve as a foundation for further planning.

Connect to the business purpose

Link objectives for the plan, explicitly, to those driving the change: keep the underlying business purpose in mind. In practice, this means you need to repeat statements about the business purpose of the change.

Adapt to the audience

Customize and interpret messages appropriately for different audiences (e.g., managers, employees, customers). Address the interests, needs, and concerns of each group.

Use multiple channels

Communicate the change summary messages in different venues, and as often and consistently as possible. Many organizations have implemented major changes with an e-mail announcement, perhaps supplemented by a conference call or meeting with a Q&A opportunity. These actions are unlikely to be sufficient to explain and embed a complex organizational change.

Listen

An important part of the communication process is to address issues, concerns, questions, and resistance. Do this through careful listening. It can be formally, through assessments and surveys, or informally, through day-to-day interaction and conversations among managers and employees. Whatever the approach, you can be sure that you're communicating in the right way and about the right issues.

Support media with process

While core information may be conveyed via e-mail or other systems, each individual will process the data in their own way, and needs time and discussion to assimilate and adapt. Interaction and conversation are important parts of shaping judgments and opinions. The process takes time—something many managers fail to recognize when pushing through change. They encounter resistance and don't realize that they created it by assuming understanding and support and moving on before the listener has absorbed, understood, and adopted the message.

Document and respond to questions

Install processes and systems for capturing and addressing questions, and ensuring that managers—or all employees—have access to this resource. If the change is complex and involves developing new roles, new skills, or other significant changes, there will be many questions. Many of these will be generated in the early stages, but others may not arise until implementation is well advanced.

Establish and track the timeline

Keep the plan on track by including deadlines and deliverables. People need to be accountable and motivated to make the change happen.

Assess and adjust

Define evaluation methods to understand what people are hearing and where they're getting the information. Ensure your communication is building the desired support and getting to the right people. Be ready to make adjustments and course corrections.

Phase 4: Compile the summary document

The primary goal at this stage is to consolidate the material developed so far and edit it into a concise summary that can be used to focus and align activities supporting the change. See Resource 3.7 (page 86) for a template with suggested structure and headings.

As you work on refining the specific messaging for the summary, have the team review it periodically. Their input and guidance will help strengthen the document. You will later be seeking detailed editorial input from a broader audience, but it's a good idea to test your ideas and approaches with your own team first.

The more feedback you get, the more challenging it can be to incorporate it all into a revised draft. Yet each element of input can strengthen the material and make it more effective for communicating to the various stakeholder groups affected by the change.

Anticipate and prepare for resistance from some of the people affected by the change, and perhaps from many of them. It's helpful to recognize this aspect of the organizational climate so that you can develop communication strategies that build confidence and win support for the change.

Your communication efforts will likely span a variety of stakeholder groups (e.g., managers, employees, customers, vendors). Following are some common scenarios you might encounter:

- Some may have heard rumors about the change, but don't understand what's happening, feel uninformed, or have been misinformed. They may perceive the change as more of a threat than an opportunity. They'll need to be reassured.
- Some may be content with the status quo and see no obvious or urgent need for change. They'll need to be convinced.
- Some may doubt the organization's ability to implement effectively. They may have seen similar initiatives fail in the past and assume this change will have the same outcome. They'll need a clear picture of how and why this will succeed.
- Some may be negatively affected (e.g., losing their jobs) and will be focused on their own concerns. It's unlikely that they can be persuaded that the change is a great idea, but they do need to understand what provisions are being made to ease the impact (e.g., transfer opportunities and/or termination benefits).

The elevator pitch: a summary of the summary

Your plan should include an elevator pitch that provides a concise and memorable snapshot of the change.

Most often, organizational change has a powerful impact on everyone involved; change generates questions, concerns, resistance. To build support and ensure a successful transition, those leading the change (sponsors, planners, and managers) must be able to communicate the important highlights of the change quickly, clearly, and consistently.

A well-formulated elevator pitch has several functions:

- It allows you to distribute core information about the change in a brief and easy-to-understand way.
- It helps managers and others be confident, consistent, and clear in responding to questions from employees.
- It provides a platform or starting point for managers and others to develop their own approach to summarizing what's going on; they can adjust and fine-tune the core pitch to adapt to their own group, team, or department.

Phase 5: Engage others to build consensus

The primary focus of this phase is to strengthen your summary draft by engaging more stakeholders for an extended review of the document. Your goal is to build alliances and gain support for the change, as well as to gather additional input that can strengthen the document.

Think of this as engaging a wide-ranging virtual team that might include people in other geographic locations, representatives of key stakeholder groups (especially ones not represented on the planning team), key organization leaders, and HR staff who will be deeply involved in the change.

> **Integrating input**
> Resource 3.5 (page 84) provides tactics for managing feedback.

Start by sharing your summary and asking for review and feedback. This provides you the opportunity to test the effectiveness of the summary, gain new perspectives, and build involvement in the change. In most cases, you can easily manage this review via e-mail.

To strengthen the review process, provide guidelines to your reviewers: tell them precisely what you're looking for in terms of feedback.

For example, discourage ambiguous responses such as "Why?", "Unclear", and "Needs to be rephrased."

If you are looking for input on only one section, state that clearly (you may send the full document for context). If you seek only a broad strategic review of the general approach, state this. But if you want detailed review and editing, clearly tell reviewers that this is what you're looking for. Be specific about when you want the feedback and in what form (e.g., on the document, with changes tracked).

Ask reviewers to consider these questions:

* Does the writing make sense; is it clear and unambiguous?
* Do the messages seem to be complete, clear, and logical?
* Does the document address concerns and objections?

Next, you want specific suggestions on how to strengthen the clarity, accuracy, and effectiveness of the document. Ask reviewers to:

* Suggest specific wording that they feel would improve clarity.
* Offer ideas about what may be missing—with suggested wording if they'd like to provide it.
* Identify new questions—along with suggested responses.

Some people seek input as a formality and treat it only cursorily. You must maintain awareness that a team can produce stronger results than an individual. Look at the input as a valued opportunity to build a much stronger document: stay open to ideas and changes.

Phase 6: Deploy the document

You need to ensure that the summary document is available to everyone who needs it to support and drive the change.

Once you've integrated the input from the extended review and refined the final draft, you're ready to distribute the document. An ideal method is to post it on an internal Web page. Make sure it's easy to find and access, and that links are posted appropriately.

Making the case
Resource 3.9 (page 93) suggests tactics for deploying the summary to make it a contributor to effective change.

As you update the material based on changes in plan or direction, or further input, post the latest version. Alert people when an updated version is available.

Keep the process alive by encouraging ongoing feedback. Continue to seek input to strengthen and update the material. Let people know the summary is a collaborative, living document, with contributions from many people, and that new input is always welcome.

Case history: Define the core message

If you don't identify the core message clearly and concisely, others will make assumptions and come up with their own ideas.

A manufacturer of office equipment was planning to distribute its products through national retailers as well as through its own stores. Initial reactions from employees were negative. They believed that maintaining control of the consultative sales process was a critical factor in their success and in the loyalty of their customers. They were not confident that staff in the retail chain could effectively and fully represent the product range and align it with the needs of customers.

The change team leader met with the CEO to clarify the business context and strategic purpose of the change. After the CEO had talked for 15 minutes, the team leader interrupted:

TL: "Can we just pause for a moment? These details are very important and I want to capture them. But what I really need from you are the core highlights—the three or four points you'd like every employee and customer to know, understand, and believe."

CEO: "That's what I'm trying to tell you . . ."

TL: "But they won't listen or read for that long, and certainly won't remember it all. They need a few short, memorable points. What do you want them to say when a family member or a customer asks them, 'What's this new sales approach? What are you trying to do with it?'"

CEO: "It's far too complex to reduce to a few sound bites."

TL: "If you don't do it, they'll make up their own or believe whatever someone else might tell them."

Bottom line: It's critical to identify the handful of core strategic points on which the change-driving document can be built—this will look very much like the elevator pitch.

RESOURCE 3.1: SAMPLE INVITATION TO JOIN THE TEAM

Follow up on initial calls with an e-mail that sets out the team's purpose and expectations for members. Start with the sample text below and adapt it as needed.

Subject: Please join the development team

Preparations for implementing *[name of initiative]* are getting started. I'd like to invite you to join a small team that *[name of executive]* has asked me to lead. Our mission is to build a summary document that will outline the changes and lay out implementation and communication plans.

Our first meeting will be *[time frame]*, with the exact date and time to be determined as soon as the membership of the team is defined.

What's the commitment?

Our task is to have the document ready for review by *[date]*. This means that we have *[number]* weeks to get this done. Starting immediately, I'm estimating you'll need to commit about *[number]* hours per week to meetings, phone calls, and e-mail communication about this work.

What's the purpose of this document?

The document will be used as a reference to guide communication, assist managers, and align the work of the various teams working on implementing the change. We'll support it with a detailed FAQ guide.

How can I deal with my current workload?

If adjustments need to be made to your workload to give you time to participate in this team's efforts, you should discuss that with your manager.[28] Let me know if can assist in this process.

Have specific roles been defined for team members?

We'll define specific roles during our first meeting. We'll also discuss our responsibilities as a team and develop a detailed plan of action.

[Add a personal note for each individual.]

---

28. Be sensitive to the workloads and relationships of those involved. A frequent cause of derailed change is the failure of the organization to recognize the extent and intensity of the added work (in addition to ongoing job demands) needed to plan and implement change.

RESOURCE 3.2: TALKING POINTS ON JOINING THE TEAM

To motivate individuals to join your team, explain what the output will mean to the organization and how the process will benefit team members. The summary below can help you explain the rationale and benefits to potential team members.

The importance of the summary document

Many change initiatives fail because the rationale is not complete or persuasive, and isn't linked to the activities, resources, and processes needed to implement it.

With a well-defined, convincing, and robust summary plan, other elements can be quickly and effectively put into place. A clear summary and high-level change plan can:

- Drive consistent messaging and reduce the need to repeatedly develop new materials.
- Exercise a forcing function early in the planning process to ensure that the case for change is clear, complete, and appropriate.
- Ensure that the purpose and process are clearly defined and fully understood.
- Help the organization communicate effectively: tell a compelling story about the change; listen to and involve those affected.
- Develop a foundation and process for building trust.

Typically, ideas and plans are not documented consistently or fully, especially during large-scale and complex change. But change provides an opportunity for you to play a broader strategic role as well as a more specific tactical one. As a member of the team, you'll be influential in defining the nature and process of the change:

- Your role will bring you in contact with key people at many levels of the organization, giving you greater awareness of the organization's culture and direction, as well as exposure to leaders.
- You'll be able to demonstrate strategic insight and leadership in the way you approach the task and in the resulting document.
- You can bring your own perspective and experience to the process, ensuring that it's well-adapted to the issues and needs of your function, team, or department.

RESOURCE 3.3: CHECKLIST OF IDEAS FOR MAKING THE CASE

The summary document needs to be persuasive and informative.[29] Present the facts and highlight benefits. Identify objections and respond to them. See below for examples of persuasive responses in discussing factors or forces that may be driving change.

Technological developments
- Describe why change is needed.
- Outline the ways in which the organization will benefit.

Growth opportunities for employees
- Identify opportunities for employee advancement; list new roles that will offer chances to build skills and careers.
- Describe opportunities for employees to train, learn, and grow.

A "burning platform"—an issue that compels action
- Describe circumstances that make change imperative, such as competition, technology, or changing customer demand.
- Be candid about the consequences of failure to change.

Business weaknesses or opportunities
- Highlight trends that require the organization to adapt to new customer needs; discuss opportunities to increase market share.

Competitive activity—a challenge to match, or an opportunity to win
- Cite facts about strengths or weaknesses in the competition. Competitive behavior is a powerful argument for change.

Customer input—what customers want and need
- Customers provide another powerful voice in the case for change, especially if they state unmet needs that a competitor can address.

Industry practices and developments
- Explain the organization's need to respond and adapt to changing industry practices, to compete in more cost-effective ways, for example, or to streamline processes based on market demands.

---

29. A useful principle, borrowed from consumer marketing, is to define an issue, demonstrate its relevance, encourage people to share the concern, and then offer a solution.

RESOURCE 3.4: GUIDELINES FOR REVIEWERS

Gathering feedback from multiple stakeholders can help to ensure accuracy, clarify language, and build support. However, the more input you get, the more challenging it can be to apply it. State that you're looking for ideas, edits, and specific language— not generalizations and questions. Start with the text below and adapt it as needed.

Subject: Request for review and comment

Attached is the first draft of the summary messaging and high-level plans for the *[name of change initiative]*. Please review the material and return your comments and suggestions to me by *[date and time]*.

Why this is important

The summary document will provide a concise description of the changes, the rationale, and the implementation process. It will provide the basis for communicating with employees and others, serve as a source document (e.g., for press releases), and act as a reference for sales staff talking with customers.

What we need from you

If you suggest changes, please be as clear as possible. Suggest wording you think would be more useful or appropriate. Avoid comments such as "this isn't clear" or "needs to be rephrased"—instead, tell us how to make it clearer or more accurate. Brevity is important: please be concise.

How you should provide your feedback

Use the Track Changes feature in Word (from the Tools menu, select Track Changes). This helps focus our work as we consolidate input.

What happens next

By *[date and time]*, we will post the document at *[URL]*. Thereafter, it will be regularly updated. Also posted will be related materials, including a set of FAQs and a summary of best practices.[30]

Your input and guidance is much appreciated. Please contact me if you have any comments or questions.

---

30. A summary of best practices is an internal benchmarking tool. It could note approaches that have been effective in managing change. It answers these questions: How are other people or organizations dealing with this? Do they have tools or ideas that we might be able to learn from or use?

RESOURCE 3.5: GUIDELINES ON MANAGING REVIEW FEEDBACK

The tactics discussed below can be useful as you work with review feedback (sometimes from multiple sources) to effectively revise and refine the summary document.

Respect and use the input

This should not be a formality. People seek input and involvement. They recognize that not every idea will be adopted but need to know their input and guidance has been considered. If you ignore input, you risk not only resistance from that individual or group, but problems with the stakeholders whose interests they were representing.

Focus on clarity and brevity

Few business documents generate complaints for their brevity, or for their clarity. Edit with care to eliminate unnecessary content and to ensure that the meaning is clear. Keep in mind the message that you want to leave the reader with, and make sure that it is delivered.

Document all questions for later use

All questions that arise out of the summary draft review should be documented as part of the process. These questions (and their answers) will help to drive other aspects of planning and may provide material for an employee FAQ guide.

Make the process open

Following input, review and revision, send the updated document to the review team. A cover e-mail should highlight key issues and the general nature of the revisions, and should express appreciation for the team's contributions. Leave the door open for continued input.

RESOURCE 3.6: WRITING FOR CLARITY AND RESULTS

Draft effective messaging for your summary document by focusing on four phases of writing: plan, draft, edit, and test. Use Word's Styles and Formatting tools, or the equivalent, to help you build a logical and clear structure, and to enable use of the Document Map feature. Styles also simplify editing and structure changes.

Plan

Consider the audience	Your readers are likely to be busy, skeptical, and under pressure. They may question, analyze, and challenge.
	Consider their expectations and attitudes; have them clearly in mind as you write.
Focus on your core message	Think through the essential meaning you want to convey.
	Talk with colleagues and others to clarify your ideas about the message and content.

Draft

Keep it short and to the point	Make it short. Avoid complex language and jargon. Split long sentences.
	Keep the writing clear, concise, and relevant.
Break up long sections	Separate long sections into two or more, and group short ones, to improve the balance of the document.

Edit

Edit for brevity	Put your core message up front. Many readers pay most attention to the first page—or the first paragraph.
	Omit superfluous words, sentences, and paragraphs. Move secondary material to appendices or linked locations.
Ensure clarity and readability	Use tables to summarize and clarify complex data.
	Highlight key points in lists, in tables, or with graphics.

Test

Test content and approach	Have people read your draft and provide feedback.
	Listen carefully to comments and make changes that address them.
Check, test and revise	Have you clearly stated what readers should know and do?
	What processes should be supporting the written material?

RESOURCE 3.7: TEMPLATE FOR THE SUMMARY DOCUMENT

This resource provides a template or framework for building your summary and business-case document. The content is organized under four broad headings: the background and purpose; the business context; details of the change; and how the transition will be accomplished. Use this as a starting point and adapt it to the needs of your change initiative.

In some cases you will write in narrative format; in others, you may use an outline format with topic sentences and bullet points. Some business case documents work well in PowerPoint, whose outlining capability encourages brief, clear exposition.

Background and purpose

Open with a brief statement of the nature and purpose of the document.

The context

This section sets the scene, outlining the state of the business and industry, mission and/or goals, and assessment of strengths and weaknesses.

Business assessment

Provide a brief summary of the organization's status, performance, and market position. The purpose is to provide the context for change. If changes are in one part of the organization (e.g., a single department), then focus on that unit.

These are examples of issues that might support the need for significant change:[31]

- The business is currently strong, but economic and other changes indicate the need for change in current processes, systems, and technology.
- The core business is under challenge (new product categories, global markets, aggressive competitors).
- The impact of changing technology requires a system upgrade to stay competitive.

Outline competitive activity, where relevant to the change. If other factors (e.g., technology, innovation, new markets, changing demographics) are influencing the change, mention those.

---

31. See page 85 for more guidance on making the case.

RESOURCE 3.7 [CONTINUED]

If business results (e.g., falling sales, lower margins, higher manufacturing costs) are driving the change, describe those.

Goal, mission, or vision

Provide a mission statement to describe the primary goal or premise of your business. If your organization does not have a mission statement, it may be appropriate to create one. Although this is itself a challenging project, it can provide a starting point, anchor, and reference for much of what follows. Make the statement brief, focused, and relevant.[32]

Build on this platform: state the specific purpose for the change and outline how it supports or strengthens the mission.

SWOT analysis

An analysis of strengths, weaknesses, opportunities, and threats (SWOT) is a valuable exercise in planning for change. First, it helps you assess issues internal to your business (strengths and weaknesses) and those that are external (opportunities and threats). From there, you can prepare strategically by determining how well your strengths align with opportunities, and where your weaknesses will be vulnerable to the threats.

Strengths that you can build on and leverage might include:

- Leading technology and services
- Resources and cash flow
- Reputation in the industry and/or community
- Respected management and ability to attract talent
- Established relationships with loyal suppliers and customers

---

32. This is typically a succinct sentence or paragraph that states the core guiding purpose of the organization. Some notable examples: "Explore the Missouri to its source and find a practicable route across the continent"; "Use the Internet to transform book buying into the fastest, easiest, and most enjoyable shopping experience possible"; "By the end of the decade, send a man to the moon and return him safely to Earth"; ". . . [be] the premier purveyor of the finest coffee in the world while maintaining our uncompromising principles."

RESOURCE 3.7 [CONTINUED]

Candidly outline weaknesses. They might include:

- Lack of new products and services
- High costs and/or low productivity
- A sales model focused more on products than solutions
- Inadequate IT infrastructure

List opportunities for the business. For example:

- New products and services in the development pipeline
- Competitors struggling with technological change
- Cost advantages based on manufacturing efficiency, outsourcing, or other strategies
- Undeveloped relationships with business partners

Describe threats that could weaken the business. Examples include:

- Emerging competition or new sources of supply
- Technological developments that could make a product obsolete
- Aggressive competitive behavior
- Government intervention and regulation

Purpose, details, and impact of the change

This core section of the document presents what's happening, why, and how implementation will be conducted.

Nature and purpose of the change

Write a brief statement that describes the change initiative. For example, explain the reorganization, new IT system, merger, sales training program, or office relocation.

Connect with and lead to the transition plan to establish a clear connection between the "why" of the change and the "how" of your plan.

RESOURCE 3.7 [CONTINUED]

Expected outcomes

The summary document should clearly describe how the change will support the stated purpose. For example:

- If the goal is greater competitiveness in a certain product category, state the way the change will affect costs, market demand, and other factors.
- If the purpose is to improve customer data available to phone-center staff, outline the nature of the data and the way it will be accessed and used.
- If the purpose is to sustain growth, describe the way the change will support that goal.

Impact of the changes

Provide examples of the way the change(s) will impact stakeholders.

- *Employees:* Uncertainty and concern about personal impact; opportunities including new roles, new skills, and opened career paths; need for training and development; adjustment to new leadership and teams.
- *Customers:* Distraction as they feel the impact of the change; possible referral to competitors; uncertainty about product availability; concerns about service and support.
- *HR specialists:* Impact on workload if changes call for time-intensive activities such as layoffs, training, or sales support; impact on accounting staff of a new inventory management system.
- *Managers:* Added workload and need for improved readiness as they build teams, develop relationships with new staff, or take on additional and/or changed responsibilities.

RESOURCE 3.7 [CONTINUED]

How the transition will be accomplished

Summarize major components of the change process. In a large-scale change, these might map to transition team subgroups.

Core elements of the transition plan

- *Readiness:* Training and education to equip people for new roles
- *Talent management:* Selection processes to identify people for open positions; development programs for longer-term growth
- *Manufacturing strategy:* Facilities integration; introduction or expansion of lean manufacturing methods; productivity improvement in parts supply and distribution
- *Team-building:* Initiatives to integrate leaders and build teamwork
- *Transition:* Procedures for handling job losses and other transitions, including termination benefits, job-search support, internal placement, or other assistance
- *Communication:* Identification of key stakeholders, summary of approaches to providing information and seeking input
- *Information:* Sources of information, guidance, and advice, including individuals or systems (such as internal Web sites)
- *Rewards:* Changes in pay and benefit programs to align with the new organization's needs
- *Technology:* Integration and evolution of computer systems

Roles, responsibilities, and timeline

- Who will be responsible for the process, and with what resources? Identify the individuals and teams who will plan and guide the transition process.
- How will the additional workload called for by implementing the change be handled, including reallocation of priorities?
- What are the major activities, steps, and milestone dates?

Metrics and review process

- What will success look like? How will it be measured?
- What processes are in place to implement course corrections?

RESOURCE 3.8: TALKING POINTS FOR CHANGE

This resource provides examples of talking points to address typical questions that arise early in the process. With any change, there are always unknowns, but don't wait until decisions are made to communicate. Even if there's a lack of clarity, discuss the context and purpose of the change, and seek input and ideas. In the absence of communication, rumor and guesswork will fill the gap. Share what you know, acknowledge what you don't know, and engage in conversation about the issues to build confidence in the process.

1. **Things are going pretty well. Why do we need to change?**

   Technology and our customers are changing, and we need to change along with them. To succeed, we need to innovate and change, stay ahead of the competition . . .

2. **This calls for new skills—how are we going to acquire them?**

   To the extent possible, positions in the new organization will be filled from inside, and we're committed to helping everyone acquire the skills they need. We expect to do some hiring for specialist roles where we don't have or can't quickly develop the right skills.

   But for most of us, this is an opportunity to develop new skills and experience. Information about training opportunities is at . . .

3. **This is going to mean a lot of extra work. Can we still take care of customers while this is happening?**

   Yes, this will indeed call for additional effort from many people as we work out the details of the transition. The plan does cover the ways we'll keep our focus on customers throughout the process *[add examples]*.

   We're asking everyone to commit to maintaining our current high standards of quality, but we'll also be outsourcing some tasks, and adding temporary staff.

   As this develops, talk with your manager about resources . . .

4. How are fewer reps going to improve customer service?

The new Customer Relationship Management (CRM) system provides far more information about each of your contacts and is easier to access and use. Calls will take less time, and will accomplish more.

You'll be able to reach customer data faster, and have the information needed to complete a sale, including history, credit card data, and shipping preferences . . .

5. I've heard that most big mergers fail. How is this different?

This brings together two groups that sell to the same market, yet with different regional strengths.

There's little overlap between the two sales forces, so we can extend the product range, strengthen our appeal, and increase sales . . .

6. We've made other acquisitions and they've generally been problematic and not very successful. Why will this work when previous efforts have failed?

This change will be handled quite differently from prior ones. For example, the process will include intensive training that was missing in earlier initiatives.

We're involving teams in the planning process, while in previous efforts planning was done centrally, and there was insufficient input from the people who were most affected.

And this time we have the IT systems to make sure we can support sales teams effectively . . .

7. What's in this for me?

You have the chance to learn and advance in a faster-growth environment with many opportunities to acquire new skills and experience, and to build your career.

You'll have access to broader and deeper resources (including training and development, career planning, and information support). A stronger business means improved job security and expanded opportunities . . .

RESOURCE 3.9: GUIDELINES ON DEPLOYING THE DOCUMENT

This resource provides tactics for sharing the finished summary document in ways that help build support and involvement for the change. With a clear and well-defined story about the change initiative, you need to ensure that the platform it provides is used. And you need to keep it under active review, updating as necessary.

Distribute to change sponsors and seek feedback

Ensure that change sponsors have the document. Be sure that they will provide feedback and details of changes that need to be included.

Ask them to use the document as a primary source when preparing material (e-mails, presentations, reports) relating to the change. This will ensure consistency in communication about the change.

Create a snapshot version: your elevator pitch

Create an elevator pitch (a three- or four-point summary). Include this in the summary document, and also distribute it separately to managers and others who will frequently be involved in discussions about the changes.

Encourage managers and others to adapt the pitch to their own local issues. They can use this when discussing the changes with their teams.

Distribute to those who interact with stakeholders

Direct the summary to the persons or groups (e.g., marketing, communication, HR staff) who manage communication with key stakeholders (e.g., employees, customers, external media, shareholders).

Ensure that materials they develop and distribute are aligned with the summary. Ask them to share with you the materials they develop.

Also invite them to give you feedback and suggestions for correcting, updating, and strengthening the content.

Track the change and be ready to update

As change develops, the issues and priorities will change. Stay aware of these, and adapt the summary as needed.

When necessary, create additional content describing progress and next steps. Keep the material current and relevant. Make sure everyone is referencing the most recent, accurate, and relevant information about the change.

RESOURCE 3.9 [CONTINUED]

Encourage feedback to strengthen the case

Let recipients know the summary is a collaborative, living document and that you welcome input to help strengthen it.

Seek feedback in a structured way after the material has been in use for a few weeks. For example, set up an online survey and ask a few brief questions to prompt feedback and ideas.

Create collateral to support and extend the summary

Additional material could include FAQ guides with answers—perhaps in versions for employees, managers, and various functional areas.

Work with your team as well as subject-matter experts to identify questions for this document and to develop crisp, clear responses.

Prepare a PowerPoint presentation for managers and others to use in briefing and planning meetings.

Invite those using these resources to send you the versions they develop so that best practices can be shared and leveraged.

Mention the resources in internal communications

As appropriate, place references in internal communication, management newsletters, and similar media.

Ask senior leaders to reference the document in their own meetings, and to encourage or require its use by others.

Stay connected to your team. Work with them to review changes and additions to the summary document. Encourage team members to continue to explore issues, needs, and solutions.

Hold periodic follow-up meetings (live or via conference call) to evaluate developments and progress and to plan responses.

Post the summary document on an internal Web page

Make the document available to everyone by posting it to an online resource page that includes the latest version and an evolving FAQ guide.

Include a field for posting questions, and a section where managers can share ideas, tactics, and experiences that will be informative and useful to others as they address the change.

Track progress and usage: evaluate the usefulness and application of the material; amend and update as indicated.

CHAPTER 4

Managing employee focus groups

BUILD CHANGE ON AWARENESS OF THE ISSUES

Gathering input from key individuals and groups—before, during, and after organizational change—is one of the keys to planning and sustaining a successful transition.

When change runs into obstacles or fails to achieve the intended impact, it's very often because of unforeseen reactions. Research to uncover and understand these is an important part of the planning process. It enables you to develop responses to objections and questions, to involve key groups in planning to address issues, and to understand and address sources of resistance.

Several factors in the framework for change outlined in Chapter 1 can be supported by research among stakeholders—including employees. The process can build engagement, establish communication priorities and needs, and identify how business systems and programs can be managed to better support change. The activity also provides a way to track the progress of a change that's already under way.

There are many ways of gathering data, ranging from simple and informal methods (casual conversations or small-group meetings) through formal and comprehensive assessments (online surveys, or team or group planning meetings). The approach you choose will depend on the nature and extent of the change, the resources and time available, and the organization's culture and management style.

Focus groups can be effective in many settings, and offer one of the most effective approaches to gathering data for change planning.

Typically, focus groups are used for research for marketing, political and other research with targeted demographic groups. But they have many other applications within organizations, and especially in the context of change management. When a business faces a major transition, employee feedback gathered via focus groups can be a powerful resource for guiding the planning process.

Focus groups are a fast and effective way of gathering information about employee beliefs, expectations, needs, and ideas. A powerful tool for change management, focus groups can achieve the following results:

- Provide information and ideas to assist leaders as they plan.
- Assess the opinions of different groups of stakeholders across the organization, quickly and cost-effectively.
- Verify or challenge assumptions about individual and group perceptions; uncover ideas and issues not previously considered.
- Identify potential or actual sources of resistance.
- Inform the organization about employee questions and concerns, and why certain opinions are held.
- Demonstrate the organization's commitment to listening to and involving employees in the planning process.
- Support and encourage other forms of engaging and involving employees in planning and change.

Focus groups generate ideas as well as questions that need to be answered. And they demonstrate a commitment to obtaining input from stakeholders. Focus groups help you anticipate issues, obstacles, and questions that help you establish realistic and effective plans for change.

Elevator pitch
See Resource 4.1 (page 111) for a concise statement that makes the case for conducting focus groups.

This chapter includes an overview that outlines the purpose and nature of focus groups, and guidance on the major steps. It also includes tools and working resources such as checklists, talking points, model agendas, communication materials, and process guides. These are designed to be adapted to your own use.

Case history: Strong rationale, weak execution

On the face of it, the acquisition held out the prospect of benefits to both organizations, with limited risk.

The strategic rationale was clear. The acquiring company, which initiated the friendly merger, held a major share of the market for CRM (customer relationship management) software in several major industrial categories. It had more than a 50 percent share among large organizations and about 30 percent in midsize, though virtually no penetration in small businesses. The acquired company was also in the business of developing, marketing, and supporting CRM software, but focused on the needs of small businesses. Their products didn't scale well for larger organizations.

The deal offered the prospect of opening up new markets for the first organization, while enabling the second to provide a new, scalable product to some of its faster-growing customers. As these customers grew in size, reach, and complexity, they tended to migrate to competitive products.

An integration task force was formed. At the first meeting, a high level of interest among employees was reported, along with some anxiety. There were concerns about whether the merger could have some unexpected negative impacts on (for example) staffing levels.

Those at the meeting were inclined to dismiss the concerns. "They don't get it—it's all about growth and success in the market," said one participant. "This gives both companies great opportunities for expanding and doing new things," said another.

A manager from the larger (and initiating) company observed that she saw things a little differently.

"I had my regular monthly team meeting last week," she said. "There was a lot of discussion about the merger, and I heard some things that surprised me. For example, someone said that they'd heard the development groups would eventually be merged—with people being let go. Someone else said that people think there'll be job losses in the sales force as well. And it was even suggested that all we want is the products, the customers, and a few of the people—and that we'll essentially just shut them down when we've taken all we want."

"There are always rumors like that," someone commented. "It's just speculation."

"But why are they speculating? Perhaps it's because we haven't told them much yet, and we assumed and hoped they'd see that this is a great deal all around."

The task force decided to undertake a fast but thorough assessment effort using focus groups to gather input, issues, questions, and ideas from key groups of employees in both organizations.

The meetings were planned and conducted in two weeks. The process involved four team members, each conducting 6 to 8 meetings. The one-hour meetings (more than 30 of them, across all three major locations) involved developers, clerical and support staff, salespeople, managers, first-level supervisors, HR team members, production and distribution staff, and others. The result was a mass of data, including hundreds of thoughtful and challenging questions, many unexpected but significant concerns, and a high level of both interest and anxiety.

The research group reported back to the task force. Intensive discussion and follow-up work ensued; the questions were addressed and the concerns assessed.

- There was no hidden agenda to merge groups and cut people—but there was a clear recognition that there might be opportunities to generate some cost savings.
- There was no plan to dismantle the smaller company or its development team—though it was recognized that there might be ways to strengthen both groups by transfers and short-term exchanges.
- There was no intent to move the smaller company's customer base to the acquiring company's sales force—but there was a plan to emphasize cross-selling that might result in some account consolidation.

So the employees' concerns did have some legitimacy, though many were founded on an incomplete understanding of the strategy. Neither organization intended large-scale job losses. But they needed to acknowledge the possibility and address the issue in an appropriate way. As well as informing that strategy, the focus groups provided much other data on which to base communication and operational planning.

The process itself demonstrated that leaders were serious about listening, aware of concerns and issues, and ready to communicate candidly about the solutions that were being developed. The merger wasn't trouble-free. But management's heightened awareness of the need for ongoing tracking and listening helped to limit concerns, and it contributed to the development of trust and constructive collaboration.

OVERVIEW OF THE FOCUS GROUP PROCESS

This section outlines the format and scope of a typical focus group process, as well as some of the key factors that can support a successful assessment effort.

Characteristics

Focus groups typically have these characteristics:

- The group consists of 6 to 12 people who respond to questions and engage in discussion about a specific topic for an hour or more.
- Participants may be selected at random or be nominated by managers. They will probably not be an intact workgroup; they may or may not know one another.
- A facilitator moderates the group discussion using prepared questions and techniques to encourage participation across the group.
- The facilitator or an assistant captures the input with note-taking and possibly audio or video recording.
- Results from each focus group are summarized and may be shared with group members for verification.
- A report details key issues, concerns, conclusions, and recommendations.
- The report is distributed to the sponsors of the process and to others in the organization who can use the data.
- Feedback and appreciation are shared with group members following each meeting.

Focus groups have some advantages over other types of feedback mechanism. They are relatively easy to arrange and conduct. You can gather a great deal of data quickly, in a setting that allows for discussion and clarification of the issues.

Keys to success

Perhaps the primary need for an effective process is to have a very clear purpose, and to communicate about this and about the way the meetings will be conducted, with participants, supervisors, and others.

- Establish a comfortable setting for the discussion (in a neutral location, if possible) and have your process well-prepared.
- Engage a trained facilitator, or at least an individual who is experienced in managing group processes and able to draw out candid feedback from employee participants.
- Verify input by sharing a summary with participants and inviting clarification and further ideas. Ensure that participants feel they are being heard and their opinions are being valued.
- Finalize a report of findings that accurately and vividly captures employees' key issues, needs, and concerns.

Within organizations, focus groups are often used in the context of a specific initiative or situation—examples include a merger, the introduction of new computer systems, changes to benefit or compensation programs, or relocation to a new facility.

State clear goals

Before embarking on the process, clearly articulate your broad purpose and specific goals. This statement will be used in discussions with management, in communication with employees and others in the organization, and in formulating questions to guide the focus group discussions.

As you draft the goals, reflect on what questions you want answered. For example, if focus groups are conducted in the early stages of the integration process following a merger, the following might be some typical issues you'd want to explore with employees:

- Expectations of the results of the merger, including questions about the purpose and process.
- Perceptions of the "other" organization's strengths, weaknesses, and culture.
- Concerns about the outcomes, including the impact on career and other opportunities.
- Information and resources needed to enable employees to operate effectively during and after the transition.

STRUCTURING FOCUS GROUPS

Some of the factors to consider in planning focus groups include group size, participant selection, meeting logistics (location, timing, and duration), communication with participants and others, facilitation, note-taking or recording, verification and follow-up, and reporting the results.

Group size

The number of participants in your groups may depend on the preferences of facilitators and the success of your recruiting efforts. Typically, a group consists of 6 to 12 members. Many consider a group of 8 to be ideal; it's easy number of participants to manage and provides leeway for each participant to have a good amount of "air time."

Having more than 10 or 12 people can make it difficult to get balanced, quality feedback from all participants. Small groups may work especially well when the role of facilitator and note-taker is combined.

Factors to consider in deciding on group size include the following:

- *The nature of the topic:* If the issue is a highly sensitive one, such as closure of an office or plant, a smaller group might encourage participants to feel safe in opening up about their true impressions and concerns.
- *The facilitator's experience:* You want quality input, not just quantity. Leading a focus group requires strong facilitation skills. Even a small group benefits from having a facilitator who can manage discussion, help everyone generate input, and stay on topic.
- *The availability of resources:* The number of focus groups conducted will be driven in part by your resources and the number of facilitators available. If one individual is to conduct all the sessions, the number of groups may be determined by how many meetings that person can schedule within a short time.
- *The quantity of feedback needed:* A large group offers less chance for each participant to provide input. But if some participants are reluctant to make a contribution, a large group ensures you will still gather a good volume of responses.
- *The importance of providing broad opportunities for input:* In some cases, you may find employees eager to take part, and larger groups will help ensure that more people can be included.

Within a day, one person can reasonably conduct four 90-minute meetings or six 60-minute meetings; and more are often squeezed into the schedule. But even four or five can be demanding, especially if the leader has limited experience facilitating such meetings. A good approach is to start with fewer sessions the first day and then step up the schedule as necessary.

Participant selection

You'll need to define the demographic profile of the sample: the overall makeup of participants for your focus groups. For example, based on employee populations, you might choose two groups from software development; two groups from operations; one group each from manufacturing, customer service, and administration; and three groups from marketing/sales.

You can then select participants at random (e.g., every eighth name on the employee roster for each part of the organization) or ask supervisors or managers to nominate people. The focus group process is designed to take a snapshot of issues and ideas. A cross section of employees from all major functions and areas will represent broad opinions effectively.

If the topic is potentially controversial, select those most directly affected by the issues. Do not shy away from people who might have critical or negative opinions: you need that feedback.

When you contact supervisors and managers to nominate participants, you can provide guidelines about what you're looking for. If you contact employees directly, be sure to tell them why they were selected (e.g., nominated by their supervisor or selected at random).

Meeting logistics

See also the Resource section of this chapter (starting on page 115) for checklists and other tools to assist you in planning and implementing focus groups.

Location

Meeting rooms should be convenient to the participants, with clear directions and other details sent out well in advance. The setting should be comfortable and quiet; a conference room is ideal. If none is available, a corner of a lunchroom (not at a meal time) can serve. Provide writing materials in case participants want to take notes.

It's a good practice to provide refreshments, especially water and other drinks. Offering lunch can serve as a useful incentive to get people to participate, but can also be a distraction from a focused discussion.

Timing

Meeting times should be set to best accommodate the schedules of the participants. If you are meeting with shift workers, minimize disruption by planning sessions for the first or last hour of the shift. In any case, consult with managers of those in the group about what works best. Facilitators should adjust their schedules, including working at night if and when necessary.

> **Stay on time**
> Whatever the duration of the meeting, clearly inform participants about the finishing time—and be sure that you finish on time or early.

Duration

Typical length for a focus group is 60 to 90 minutes. Ninety minutes allows time for all participants to share in the discussion. But 60 minutes may be sufficient when you have a large number of groups and can count on plenty of feedback. A facilitator can handle about six one-hour meetings in a full day, with short breaks.

Schedule 15 to 30 minutes between meetings. This provides ample time for transitions between groups, and gives the facilitator a break. It also allows time to prepare the room again, including clearing trash, restocking refreshments, and clearing the white-board or installing fresh flip charts. It can also provide some time for the note-taker to review notes and reflect on any changes of approach.

Communication with participants and others

Focus groups may generate a high level of interest, curiosity, and even concern. Careful communication is important to clarify the purpose, to reassure participants and others about what's happening and why, to explain why some will participate and others will not, and to address operational issues including time away from the job.

Managers must know about the process and why individuals in their groups may be asked to participate. They need to be equipped with responses to questions from invited participants. For example, people might ask, "Why me?"

If the selection is random, the manager can tell them so and explain the purpose. If the person is being nominated, the manager will need to explain that the aim is to identify people within a certain group who have opinions and feel comfortable expressing them. In either case, people not initially included who express a strong interest in the process can and should be invited to take part.

> **Send a reminder**
> Send a reminder e-mail the day before the scheduled focus group. Restate the purpose, location, time, and duration.

Inform nonparticipating employees about the process and why their colleagues may be attending meetings. You may also want to offer them a channel for providing input of their own. This can be done with a Web page where they can ask their own questions, raise issues, or offer ideas. Or you can give them a questionnaire (on-line or on paper) based on the focus group outline.

FACILITATING FOCUS GROUPS

You may find experienced facilitators in your HR or training departments, in organizational development groups, or elsewhere within the organization.

In some cases you may want to look outside for professional facilitators to lead focus groups. An effective hybrid approach (where budget is an issue but in-house resources aren't available) is to engage a facilitator to conduct the first few groups. You can observe and learn, and then conduct the rest of the groups yourself.

In all but the smallest group sessions, it's ideal to have two people running the session. One can lead the discussion while the other takes notes and/or monitors any recording equipment. Partnering in this way enables the facilitator to stay focused on managing the flow of conversation and participation, while someone else keeps track of recording the group's responses and observations.

In practice, resource limitations mean that many focus group efforts are handled with the leaders managing the discussion as well as taking notes. This can be effective as long as preparation is thorough and a suitable note-taking strategy is employed.

The primary goal of the focus group process is to obtain useful, informative feedback from participants. To get that, you must help people feel comfortable enough to speak candidly. Address questions that are relevant and important to them, give them ample opportunity to express their opinions, and leave them feeling confident that their input will be heard and acted on.

In addition to obtaining valid data, you want the process itself to leave a positive impression on participants. If the discussion is not well-managed (for instance, if a few people dominate the discussion or key issues are left unaddressed), participants might be left with a negative impression. This may erode or reverse the focus group's value to the organization.

Framework and process

The facilitator should work with a discussion guide that outlines the key questions and issues to be addressed. Major elements should include an introduction, core questions, and notes for closing the meeting.

The introduction will include a clear statement of the purpose of the assessment, a description of the process, an assurance of confidentiality, and a review of next steps.

Here are the elements of a well-facilitated discussion.

Welcome participants and set the scene

Greet people and thank them for attending. Introduce yourself to the group; outline the purpose and agenda for the session. Explain the follow-up process, and encourage open and candid discussion.

Provide reassurance that the discussion will be confidential (e.g., "no participant names will be included in reports, and no comments will be presented in a way that enables the contributor to be identified").[33]

List core questions to be explored—on a flip chart or whiteboard. This helps keep the agenda on track as discussion proceeds.

Initiate the discussion

Engage the entire group by inviting a brief opening comment from each person. Formulate a broad question that's easy for everyone to answer comfortably (see page 117). Then continue with your planned questions.

---

33. Assurance of confidentiality is important, and expected. In some cases, where the topic is highly sensitive, success may depend on the group's acceptance that opinions will not be associated with any individual. But in many cases—perhaps the majority—participants are comfortable expressing opinions, often including critical and negative ones. "I don't mind who hears this—I'm not afraid of saying what I think" is a frequent observation.

Questions should be carefully formulated, and there should not be too many: six to eight may be sufficient.

Probe responses and explore key issues that emerge. Watch the clock and keep the discussion focused. Allow some freedom for participants to explore tangents, but try to tactfully limit these digressions. And refer to the agenda of core questions if needed.

Summarize and close the meeting

Close with an informal summary of some of the themes and main points that emerged in the meeting. Remind the group of the follow-up process including (if appropriate) their opportunity to review a summary of the discussion.

Finish on time and close by thanking the group.

Note-taking

Having an accurate account of the feedback is the fundamental goal of focus groups. It's useful to have a designated recorder as well as a facilitator. Here are some note-taking approaches you might consider.

Visible note-taking

You can incorporate note-taking into the session itself, recording discussion highlights in a way that's visible to the participants—for instance, on a flip chart, whiteboard, or overhead projector. This creates an atmosphere of openness and trust, and participants can comment or challenge as appropriate.

Generally, notes taken in this way can be easily transcribed, with minimal editing, to provide a concise summary of the session.

> **Try a dress rehearsal**
> It's helpful to practice a focus group discussion in advance. Enlist team members to act as participants or put a pilot group together. Test-drive the timing and flow of the meeting.

Standard note-taking

The note-taker can write or type notes in a way that isn't immediately accessible to the participants. In this case, it can be useful to occasionally pause and read back or otherwise verify some of the notes—and invite comment and confirmation.

A very effective way to extend and validate the process is by adding a feedback loop: following the meeting, distribute a summary to participants and ask for verification and/or correction.

Audio recording

Having an audio recording can be helpful. It can supplement your notes, ensure an accurate account, and allow you to transcribe comments verbatim. If the topic is sensitive, recording may somewhat limit the free flow of discussion.

Video recording

Video is often used in market research applications, but much less often in internal organizational settings. While it can provide compelling and useful source material for communicating findings, people may feel inhibited when being videotaped. But if the group is carefully prepared and well-facilitated, responses can still be open and useful.[34]

Verification and follow-up

Draft a summary of notes from each session and share the summary with participants for verification. Then prepare a report of findings, and distribute and follow up as necessary.

The summary of each group can be brief, focusing on the key points, especially those on which there was broad consensus. It might be no more than one to two pages of summarized findings, with an additional page or two of verbatim comments to reinforce ideas and vividly represent employee involvement.

Promote confidence in the process
Ask participants to review a summary of the session. This communicates a commitment to understand their input and to take it seriously.

For brevity and clarity, and sometimes to preserve anonymity,[35] you might need to edit or paraphrase verbatim comments. Do so sparingly and carefully: it's important that participants reviewing the summary do not feel that their comments have been misconstrued or taken out of context.

---

34. In video recording of focus groups on controversial topics (leadership style, product quality, and failure of restructuring) participants, once adjusted to the setting and equipment, often show remarkable readiness to express themselves with complete candor.
35. For example, when participants name themselves or others.

This may simply be a matter of removing repeated words or phrases—or interjections ("er," "well," "you know")—while preserving the tone and style. You need to retain the original voice for the report to remain authentic. If you do edit verbatim comments, be sure to mention this editing in the summary, so that participants are aware that comments have been paraphrased for clarity or anonymity.

Before relaying any findings to the sponsors of the process (typically, management and other groups involved in or directing the change), you should verify the summary with the focus group participants. Distribute each summary to the relevant group participants, with a note of thanks and a request for corrections and clarifications.

Participants typically display a healthy skepticism about how their input will be used. This review step can be effective in promoting confidence in the process. It enables participants to see what's being noted and feel they've been heard; it allows them to correct inaccuracies or add clarification; and it encourages them to feel involved in a larger process.

Typically only a few people offer additional input. However, the chance to review and comment is welcomed and reinforces the perception of an open and positive process. This feedback step also establishes a communication link that can be used later—for example, to test plans and ideas that are developed during the process.

Reporting the results

Once you have verified summaries for all groups, you are ready to compile the information and prepare a report of findings. This will be distributed to the sponsors of the process (and possibly other key players in the change initiative). It may also be shared with a wider audience across the organization.

> **Get the most out of summary reviews**
> When you distribute the summary, include a cover e-mail that gives participants guidelines on the type of feedback you need.

The report will highlight key issues, concerns, areas of consensus, conclusions, and recommendations. To ensure credibility and authenticity of the findings, the report should provide an accurate account of employee sentiments, including those that are critical of the direction or process of change.

It's useful to include verbatim comments in the report (as well as in session summaries). They provide lively and convincing commentary in the voices of focus group participants. Sometimes these comments are the best way of expressing a point of view or an idea.

Here are suggested elements for the report:

- *Introduction:* Clarify the purpose of the focus groups, and outline the process used, including the verification loop.
- *Overview:* Provide highlights of key issues, concerns, and themes, as well as important new ideas introduced by the group.
- *Details:* Summarize the findings by major issue categories, such as primary areas of concern, areas of consensus, and prominent new issues that surfaced.
- *Conclusions:* Close the report with a brief summary of overall results, and provide recommendations for next steps.
- *Appendix:* Include selected verbatim comments.

You now have a report that outlines issues, interests, questions, and concerns for major groups of employees (or other stakeholders). This will provide information and guidance to the individual or team planning and managing the process of change.

Those responsible for the change process can draw on the report in their planning and in preparing communication material (FAQs, training modules for managers, briefing notes for others).

Well-conducted focus groups—as with other forms of stakeholder assessments—provide a foundation of insight and knowledge on which to build effective plans to guide and support change.

Case history: Flexibility can harness energy

A focus group among telecommunications workers became heated. The questions were coming from the group rather than from the facilitator. The tone of the discussion was challenging and hostile, and focused on the perceived misdeeds of leadership. Why were jobs being lost when other departments were hiring? Why weren't workers being retrained to handle new technology? Why had there been no base pay increases?

The facilitator was trying to get discussion back to the intended topic: the introduction of a new managed-care medical plan offering improved benefits but limited choice of providers. The mention of cost as one of the drivers for the plan had triggered the group's shift of focus.

The facilitator spoke: "Okay, I understand that the business context is an important part of this. The plan has cost saving as one of its major goals; and you're concerned that the need for this is caused in part by actions you think leaders should or shouldn't be taking. You've got as many questions and concerns about that as you do about the new health care proposals.

"Let's agree to do this: we'll take another 15 minutes to talk about the broader issues and for you to lay out your concerns and questions. And then give me 15 minutes for brainstorming on questions, issues, concerns, and ideas about the health care plan."

The group agreed to the approach. The participants vented on the broader issues, with their input duly recorded by the facilitator. This proved to be a useful by-product of the process. They were then ready to be steered back to the health care issues that were the intended topic for the focus group.

At the end of the session, the group felt they'd had an opportunity to express themselves. They also felt that they had been heard. The facilitator had the input needed—as well as some additional material.

RESOURCE 4.1: ELEVATOR PITCH FOR FOCUS GROUPS

These brief talking points provide a framework for quick and informal discussions promoting the value and importance of focus groups. The context of the sample text, for illustration purposes, is a merger. Adapt these talking points to the specifics of your change initiative.

Why we're conducting focus groups

In the next two weeks, we'll be conducting focus groups in several locations. These are designed to gather information to guide the integration of the two businesses.

Focus groups will enable us to gather information about employee beliefs, expectations, needs, and ideas quickly and effectively. The meetings will provide data and insights that will help us manage the change.

The process will also demonstrate that we're committed to listening to our people and involving them in the planning process.

We'll identify issues and concerns that need to be addressed throughout the change process—for example, in manager training, information systems, relocation policies, merging of operations, and communication with employees.

These meetings will be the first phase in a continuing process of information exchange. We intend to continue and extend the dialog. We'll will ensure that all employees have an ongoing opportunity to ask questions, express opinions, and offer ideas.

RESOURCE 4.2: CHECKLIST FOR FOCUS GROUP LOGISTICS

This checklist provides a framework for planning focus groups. Use it as a guide to remind you about the major components of the process.

Item	Status

Objectives

Identify the primary purpose of the focus groups (e.g., understand attitudes and expectations relating to a merger).

List goals and assessment topics (e.g., knowledge of the other organization; expectations about outcomes; stakeholder concerns, questions and ideas).

Note how you intend to use the findings (e.g., individuals and groups who will review and act on results, products—such as an FAQ guide—that might result).

Participants

List functions, geographic areas, and employee groupings (e.g., first-level supervisors) that should be represented in the focus group process.

Determine approximate numbers of people in each category as a guide to proportionate numbers of focus groups for each. Also note groups not directly involved in the change process that should be included in the assessment process.

Identify a target group size and begin to build a sample (e.g., three groups from each major geographic area; two from each functional area; one of managers).

Scheduling

Identify meeting location(s)—which locations; available rooms in each; time and size constraints; accessibility for participants.[36]

Decide on setup of meeting facilities, including tables, supplies, and refreshments. Clarify responsibility for reserving and preparing rooms.

Determine times and duration of meetings, allowing for travel time, shift patterns, other activities at that location, and feasible number of meetings for each day.

---

36. For some groups (e.g., sales staff who rarely come to the office), arranging a meeting can be challenging. One approach is to attach this meeting to another activity that's already been scheduled—such as a monthly sales meeting. Such a "limpet" meeting is a good use of time and availability. Focus groups can also be conducted via conference call.

RESOURCE 4.2 [CONTINUED]

Item	Status
Note-taking and verification	
Determine the approach to note-taking—by the facilitator(s) or by a separate note-taker.	
Decide on recording methods (e.g., equipment needed/desired, availability, costs).	
Determine an approach to verification (e.g., if articipants have a chance to review and comment on notes from the meeting they attend).	
Define the format and timing for completion of meeting summaries.	
Reporting	
Make an initial determination of the scope and format of the report (this may change based on the outcomes of the process).	
Determine responsibility for report compilation.	
Establish timing for report development, review, and delivery.	
Determine who the report will go to, how it will be used, and what follow-up processes will be needed.	
Process management	
Plan communication about the focus group process— determine who needs to be informed and involved.	
Establish a budget and an approach to managing it.	
Seek and obtain necessary approvals.	

RESOURCE 4.3: SAMPLE E-MAILS FOR PLANNING FOCUS GROUPS

This resource includes suggested text for e-mails used to notify supervisors and others, invite participants, inform other employees, and invite participant feedback on meeting summaries. The context of the sample text, for illustration purposes, is a merger. Adjust this and other content as appropriate.

To: Supervisors and managers

We're planning to conduct a series of employee focus groups to assess progress, issues, and needs relating to the merger with *[organization name]*. We would like one (or more) of your employees to take part.

The scope of the discussions will include:

+ Understanding of the purpose of the merger
+ Effectiveness of the integration process
+ Unanswered questions
+ Extent and usefulness of support, resources, or training
+ Obstacles that need to be addressed.

These focus groups will be conducted by *[name]* between *[date and date]*. They will cover a cross-section (all functional areas and levels) of our people. You may be included in one of the management groups.

Each group will consist of people at the same level. The sessions will last for up to an hour. We appreciate your help in arranging for members of your team to attend (a total of about *[number]* randomly selected employees will be involved).

We realize that in some cases it may be difficult to release an individual and we appreciate any effort you can make to allow people to attend the sessions. This process is an important part of the integration follow-up. If you can't release someone, please let *[name]* know. We may ask you to nominate a substitute.

Following each focus group session, a summary of notes will be compiled and distributed to the participants of that group to allow them to verify or correct the conclusions. After these reviews, when a larger analysis has been completed, a report of findings will be prepared.

Confidentiality will be strictly maintained: no names will be in the report, and no comments or data will be associated with individuals.

Thanks in advance for your support of this important process. Please let *[name]* know if you have any comments or questions.

RESOURCE 4.3 [CONTINUED]

To: Focus group participants (invitation to participate)

We're planning to conduct a series of employee focus groups to assess progress, issues, and needs relating to the merger with *[organization name]*. We would like you to participate in one of these sessions.

The scope of the discussions will include:

- ♦ Understanding of the purpose of the merger
- ♦ Effectiveness of the integration process
- ♦ Unanswered questions
- ♦ Extent and usefulness of support, resources, or training
- ♦ Obstacles that need to be addressed.

These groups will cover a cross-section (all functional areas and levels) of employees. Each group will consist of people at the same level—no one will be in a group with someone they report to. The sessions will last for up to an hour.

We would like you to participate in a group scheduled for *[time]* on *[date]*. Your manager has been asked to make any arrangements needed to enable you to take part. No preparation is necessary.

This effort is an important part of the merger integration process. Please let *[name]* know by *[date]* whether you are able to attend or not. It's important that we have enough time to invite someone else if you cannot participate.

Following the meetings, notes will be distributed to the members of each group to allow them to verify or correct the conclusions.

Confidentiality will be strictly maintained: no names will be in the report, and no comments or data will be associated with individuals.

Thanks in advance for your support of this important process. Please let *[name]* know if you have any comments or questions.

RESOURCE 4.3 [CONTINUED]

To: All employees (information)

We're planning to conduct a series of employee focus groups to assess progress, issues, and needs relating to the merger with *[organization name]*. The scope of the discussions will include:

- Understanding of the purpose of the merger
- Effectiveness of the integration process
- Unanswered questions
- Extent and usefulness of support, resources, or training
- Obstacles that need to be addressed.

The groups will cover a cross-section (all functional areas and levels) of *[company name]* employees. Each group will consist of people at the same peer level—no one will be in a group with someone they report to. The sessions will last for up to an hour.

If you are not included in one of the groups but would like to contribute your ideas, please contact *[name]* and we will arrange for you to receive a questionnaire based on the focus group topics.

To: Focus group participants (invitation to review meeting notes)

Many thanks for your participation in the focus group discussion at *[time]* on *[date]*. We very much appreciate the candid, thoughtful, and useful input the group provided.

Attached is a summary of notes from your session which reflect key points from the discussion. I'd like to ask you to review the summary and make any corrections or additions you feel are relevant. Summaries from all the groups will be incorporated into an overall report of findings we are preparing for *[name or group]*.

If the summary seems complete there's no need to respond.

If you would like to offer suggestions or corrections, please get them back to me by *[date]*. It would be helpful if you would add them directly to the document. If you're familiar with the Track Changes feature of Word, using that will be helpful. But feel free to make notes in any form you wish, or to simply send an e-mail with your comments.

Again, your input and guidance is much appreciated. Please let *[name]* know if you have any questions.

RESOURCE 4.4: TEMPLATE FOR A FOCUS GROUP GUIDE

This resource provides guidance through the steps of conducting a focus group. Included is suggested commentary that's framed, for illustration purposes, in the context of a merger. Adapt as necessary to address the needs and issues of your own project.

Welcome participants and introduce the purpose

Break the ice by greeting people as they arrive and thanking them for attending. Introduce yourself and invite them to help themselves to refreshments.

Start the session by introducing yourself to the group, thanking them for their time and participation, and clarifying the purpose of the focus group:

"Thanks for taking the time to come to this session. I'd like to take a moment to remind you why we're here, and to see if there are any questions.

"My name is [name]. I've been asked by [executive name] to gather input and ideas from employees across the organization. The purpose is to help us in the process of planning the integration effort as the merger with [organization name] moves ahead.

"As you already know, there'll be quite a few changes as we build the new organization. We want to be sure we fully understand employee needs and concerns; we very much want to have your input and ideas about how we can make this merger a success."

Here you can add a preliminary ice-breaking question:

"Does this assessment seem like a good idea—is it worth doing?"

This offers an early opportunity for participants to say something. It can provide reinforcement to the group (and to you); it can also provide early warning of issues that might derail the process.

Outline the group process and agenda

Explain the process for the discussion. Encourage participants to be candid about concerns, perceptions, and ideas:

"Here's the process: we'll spend an hour or so discussing a series of questions about the merger and the integration plans that are taking shape. I'm sure you have many questions, but I do want to stress that today's purpose is to gather input and ideas from you, rather than responding to questions.

RESOURCE 4.4 [CONTINUED]

"To the extent that you do have questions that need to be answered, we'll record those and build them into the communication plans and materials that are being prepared.

"And of course I'll be open to input not covered by our questions, if it's relevant to the overall purpose. If you have ideas that seem important but that I don't ask about, please let me know."

Outline the follow-up process; explain how feedback will be used:

"Once we've completed these meetings, we'll prepare brief summaries for each group. You'll see the summary from this meeting and will have the opportunity to correct it or add to it. The purpose of this feedback loop is to make sure that we do an effective job of capturing your input."

Assure confidentiality

"Let me assure you that no names will be used in our notes or report. Comments will be presented in a way that doesn't enable the person to be identified.

"We encourage you to be open and direct. By all means, be critical if that's appropriate, but we also encourage you to provide ideas for improvement.

"Are there any questions or concerns before we get started?"

Open the discussion

List core questions to be explored—on a flip chart or whiteboard. This helps keep the agenda on track as discussion proceeds.

Start with a broad, open-ended question that's easy to answer comfortably. Engage the entire group by going around the table and inviting a brief comment from each person. This is a nonthreatening way of encouraging everyone to say something early in the session.

Here's a useful discussion starter:

"Let's start with a broad view of [organization name] and what it's like to work here. Then we can look more closely at the possible impact of the merger, what we need to preserve, and what we should change.

"I want you all to think about a word or phrase that best describes what it's like for you here. It might be good, bad, or neutral, the response you'd give to a friend who asks, 'What's it like to work for [organization name]?'

"We'll go around the table and give everyone a chance to comment. Later we'll get into more detail."

RESOURCE 4.4 [CONTINUED]

Many people feel uncomfortable being the first to talk. You might start with the person closest to you, implying you'll move in sequence. This gives people a sense of structure for this first exercise, and they'll clearly know when they're expected to offer comment. Or pick someone who is clearly eager to speak up.

Responses are usually varied and instructive. You'll get some one-word answers (e.g., stressful, fast, chaotic, fun, boring, exciting) as well as some longer ones. Encourage people to keep it brief.

When everyone has made a contribution, begin to ask follow-up questions. If a participant is reluctant to comment ("I can't really think of anything") or seems very uncomfortable, say, *"That's fine, if something occurs to you later, feel free to let me know,"* and move on.

Continue with your planned questions
Your questions should be carefully formulated and direct. Here are some possible sample questions:

- *Issues:* *"What are your concerns about the process so far?"*
- *Information:* *"What information do you still need?"*
- *Opportunities:* *"How we can make the most of this merger?"*
- *Resources:* *"What resources (e.g., time, funds, people, systems) do you need to be able to support the change effectively?"*
- *Ideas:* *"Can you suggest ways to make it more effective?"*

Follow up and explore key issues that emerge
The discussion will very likely uncover issues of great interest and concern. As well as noting these, you will have to decide, on the spot, which to explore further with follow-up questions.

Follow-ups are very important for uncovering greater meaning behind responses. Use phrases like these:

"Tell me a bit more about the issues . . ."
"Is there anything more we should know about . . ."
"Can you give me an example of . . ."
"I need an idea of what you mean by . . ."

RESOURCE 4.4 [CONTINUED]

Manage the process

Watch the clock and keep the discussion focused. Allow some freedom for participants to explore tangents, but try tactfully to limit these digressions. For example:

"I'm going to interrupt here—this is interesting, but I want to be sure the others have an opportunity to add their comments."

Refer to the agenda of core questions, if necessary.

See Resources 4.5 and 4.6 on pages 121 and 123 for guidance on generating useful input, and on dealing with interruptions, digressions, and distractions.

Close the discussion

Before closing, ask for final observations or ideas. You want people to leave feeling that the process has been productive and meaningful, and that they've had a satisfying chance to be heard.

"I'd like us to leave the session feeling we've covered the most important and relevant topics. Is there anything we missed?"

"Is there anything else you think I should be asking?"

"Does anyone have any final thoughts they want to add?"

"This is a very helpful step forward and I appreciate your involvement today. You've given us some excellent feedback and useful ideas . . ."

Add a reminder of the follow-up process. If you will be sending a summary, discuss expectations:

"You certainly don't have to respond—if the summary seems to capture the highlights of what we discussed, that's great. But If there's anything important you think I missed, or additional ideas that occur to you, please add them."

Finish on time and close the discussion by thanking the group.

RESOURCE 4.5: TACTICS FOR GENERATING USEFUL INPUT

The tactics here include techniques for encouraging interaction, keeping the discussion balanced and positive, reaching consensus, and building involvement. An important role of the facilitator is to create an environment in which people feel relaxed and confident about speaking their minds in front of others. Participants should also leave the session with a positive attitude about the process. Build this positive attitude with encouragement, and humor.

Encourage diverse opinions and ideas

Some people will be reticent if their ideas or experiences are quite different from other views expressed in the group. But that divergence can shed useful light on an issue, and you want it to be expressed.

Reassure people that their ideas, even if not shared by others in the group, may be representative of many others in the organization.

Seek group consensus on a broad, general idea

You might explore knowledge and understanding of the organization's mission, vision, values, and goals. This tactic also helps to inform you about the group's frame of reference about the organization, which influences the perceptions, attitudes, and ideas you'll hear from them later.

"In your view, what is [organization name]'s mission?"

"What do think are the values that [organization name] operates by?"

"In what ways do you feel the mission is supported by the way the organization operates? And in what ways is it not?"

"How many of you feel this way about . . ."

Encourage interaction among participants

Encourage people to compare ideas and experiences:

"You both work in a similar situation. In what ways do you each think the merger process could be improved?"

"I'd like you all to take a few minutes to talk among yourselves and together come up with your ideal solution for making the merger work. I'm just going to sit back and listen for a bit."

Introduce subtopics to help people organize their ideas

Introduce a topic, ask for quick comments, and then work into more detail so people can offer depth, stories, and clarification.

RESOURCE 4.5 [CONTINUED]

For example, ask about communication, and then invite comments on specifics such as face-to-face communication by managers, formal communication tools (the Web or newsletters), information about the state of the business, and communication about the change initiative.

"Looking at communication, tell me how you'd rate it, and why."

"Comment on communication about the merger so far."

Prompt, encourage, and balance the discussion

If someone offers an idea and then grows quiet, provide some prompts:

"Tell me more . . ."

"Okay, keep going . . . this is helpful . . ."

Give everyone an opportunity to contribute. Try to draw in those who have been quiet—without pushing to the point where they become uncomfortable. Keep discussion balanced by encouraging people who haven't had much or any chance to contribute. But be sure to let reserved people know that it's okay not to have or express an opinion:

"Let's hear a different perspective on that."

"Let's see, we haven't heard from . . ."

"Can anyone add to this idea?"

To learn about how people see the organization or a topic, brainstorm strengths and weaknesses:

"Let's brainstorm around people-related strengths. What are the best characteristics of the organization? What can we build on?"

"Now let's talk about the areas where [organization name] *needs to improve—again, related to people and especially to these changes."*

Seek potential solutions for resolving issues

You don't want participants to feel they have to provide solutions for the organization, but probe them for ideas on what they would like to see happen, what they need that they aren't getting, and so forth:

"If you could make one change to the process, what would it be?"

Reiterate what you're hearing to have the group verify it.

Active listening involves responding with a brief recap, to reassure the group that you listened and to verify that you understand:

"I want to make sure I've got this. What you're saying is . . ."

"So the message I should take away from your story is . . ."

RESOURCE 4.6: GUIDELINES ON MANAGING RESISTANCE

The tactics below can help you deal with issues and challenges that might arise during a focus group discussion—including participants who are inclined to dominate discussion, or those who are reluctant to contribute.

Someone who is reluctant to talk

You might draw a comment from a passive participant by a direct question—though in an encouraging tone rather than a directive one:

"You haven't said much yet, but I'm sure you have some great ideas."

"I'd really like to hear your take on this."

Another approach is to use a break to talk with the person privately, and ask them if they'd be prepared to share their ideas with the group.

But you shouldn't apply significant pressure for someone to talk. One of your goals is for participants to leave the session with a positive impression. You want them to feel that you asked the right questions and listened carefully; and that the discussion was useful and respectful. You rarely have a group in which everyone participates actively.

Someone who doesn't align with the group consensus

If a participant has an opinion, belief, or perspective that is decidedly different from the majority, explore that difference. Ask questions to open discussion of the issue. Explore the divergent points of view:

"Does anyone else feel the same way?"

"That's an interesting point of view, and a bit different from some of the other things we've heard. Who'd like to add a comment?"

A participant who is adept at articulating a position (even if it's subjective) can sometimes sway the beliefs of the group. Ask the person to explain why they hold that position and probe further to help the group distinguish between a logical idea and someone's personal agenda:

"Can you share some examples of how it's happened and why?"

Participants who have a separate conversation

Side conversations are more likely to occur if the discussion is slow, the subject matter is of low interest, or one or two people are doing most of the talking. Try to address those problems, but also address the issue directly. Generally, other participants will appreciate the intervention:

"Can we focus on having just one discussion? And if you have other ideas or input, by all means share them with the group."

123

Discussion that seems to be slowing to a halt

Sometimes the reluctance to engage and to offer opinions seems to extend to an entire group. Be sure that you have plenty of questions in reserve to try to find an area that generates interest and a response. You can also change direction and introduce a fresh topic:

"We seem to have covered everyone's ideas about how to make the new structure work effectively. Let's move to another important topic: how we can keep customers happy and limit any concerns they may have about the changes."

Someone who dominates the discussion

This type of participant can easily derail the group by robbing others of the opportunity to comment, or even intimidating other participants.

Address this directly by courteously describing the behavior:

"Thanks for your comments, [name]. You certainly feel strongly about this, and it's useful to get your point of view. But I think you're taking more than an even share of the time, and I do want to hear from everyone else. So is it okay if we let the others provide their ideas and input for a while?"

Another approach to getting things back on track is to move to a more structured approach. You can restrict the free-flowing conversation and instead ask people to speak in turn, going around the table:

"I do want to hear from everyone. So let's go around and I'll ask you each to give me a 60-second summary—just two or three quick thoughts on how we could better prepare for the merger."

Disagreement or conflict among participants

A useful first step in addressing problems with the process is to describe clearly what you see happening. This is reassuring to those in the group who aren't engaged in negative behavior; it also lets those disagreeing know the effect that their actions are having.

"This discussion is getting heated, and I think the emotions are taking over. There's nothing wrong with disagreement—in fact it's helpful for me to hear the various points of view—but let's try to cool it down a bit and keep the discussion rational and respectful."

"Let me try to understand why this issue seems to be generating some conflict here. What you're saying is . . ."

If necessary, move the discussion on to another topic:

"Let's move away from that for a while and come back to it when we've gathered some more input."

CHAPTER 5

Developing and managing a change planning workshop

ENGAGE KEY CONTRIBUTORS IN PLANNING FOR CHANGE

This chapter contains material to assist you in developing and conducting a planning workshop for a team responsible for implementing a major change initiative. Such a workshop can be a key step toward building an organization-wide plan to implement change. It can support several of the core factors in successful change, including clarity, engagement, communication, alignment and tracking.

Examples of changes that a workshop might play a part in planning include a restructuring, merger or acquisition; a geographic expansion; cultural change; deployment of new systems; changes in role and reporting relationships or in reward systems; and office or plant relocations.

If the process is designed well and the team is fully engaged, such a workshop can enable the basic elements of a plan to be developed rapidly and effectively. The process reinforces team-building through addressing the challenges and realities of implementing and sustaining change.

Starting on page 143 you will find a variety of resources (including agendas, checklists, session directions, and other tools) for you to adapt and deploy in your own organization. As in the rest of this book, the material can be adapted to reflect the circumstances of the change; the nature of the organization; the needs and characteristics of participants; and leadership philosophy, style, and strategy.

> **Generic meeting-planning templates**
>
> The frameworks in this chapter are designed to assist in planning workshops to address change. But they can provide a useful starting point for other kinds of meetings, including those for annual planning, leadership, or team-building.

WORKSHOP APPROACHES

There is a broad spectrum of approaches to workshops and planning meetings. They range from participative to directive; from informal and unstructured to highly planned and tightly managed.

- *A participative approach* imposes minimal constraints or directions. The team is presented with a challenge (e.g., strengthen customer service; reduce energy costs; build teamwork) and with the freedom (though not always the resources) to address it.[37]
- *A midlevel approach* is participative but with a clear structure. Meeting attendees have the opportunity to discuss, reflect, ask questions, offer feedback, and influence the change process. At the same time, there is clear direction and oversight for the planning and process of the meeting.
- *A directive approach* (top-down) is primarily an information exchange; participants receive instructions, training, and tools.

The approach you choose will depend on many factors, including your organization's culture. The way change is planned should model the values and processes of the change itself. This chapter focuses on a midlevel approach that blends direction and clear leadership with active problem-solving and a high degree of participant involvement.

DEFINING THE PURPOSE AND SCOPE

Use the questions below as a preliminary step to review your goals, consider who should be involved, and begin to define the approach:

- Is the overall purpose and shape of the change process defined?
- What role do you want the change planning team to play?
- What decisions will the participants have power to influence?
- How much diversity of opinion do you anticipate?
- How does the organization typically plan for change, and how should that influence process design?

---

37. Many business meetings operate under this undirected model, in part because the leader is unwilling or unable to impose a structure or process. Attractive and democratic though this might seem, some facilitation or meeting discipline is generally needed. Time and resources may be better managed, and there may be a greater likelihood of reaching or creating conclusions, decisions, or plans.

- How skilled at managing conflict and diversity of ideas are you or others who might share workshop leadership?
- Do you expect to brief workshop participants on the approach to change, or have them develop plans?
- Will the focus be largely on sharing information, or will you be seeking significant input and guidance?
- Would you like participants to become agents for the change (i.e., to become key focal points in leading, modeling, and supporting the change)?
- Are you ready to accept push-back and perhaps rethink some or many aspects of the planned change?
- What do you want to happen as a result of the workshop?

Following are guidelines to help make the process a success:

- *Lay the groundwork:* Pre-workshop activity (such as a brief survey) is very useful in laying the groundwork, managing expectations, and adapting the workshop to the needs of the participants.
- *Foster involvement:* Tactics during the workshop should aim for a high level of involvement from participants. Tactics may include use of breakout groups and other participative activities.[38]
- *Provide feedback:* Feedback to participants can include summaries of decisions, questions, and ideas. Provide these during and after the workshop to test and reinforce conclusions.
- *Facilitate with balance:* Disciplined yet flexible facilitation—a difficult but feasible blend—moves through the agenda purposefully while allowing for and adjusting to challenges and new issues.
- *Follow up:* Post-workshop reporting, including confirmation of decisions, maintains momentum and retains engagement.

---

38. This is a broad term referring to any process in which you split the group into two or more smaller subgroups. In some cases this may be as simple as assembling people around each end of a conference table. In a larger room or auditorium, people can form groups—moving chairs as needed—within the same room. Or separate meeting rooms can be allocated: people then leave the meeting room and reconvene in their groups. The process can range from entirely informal ("form groups and spend five minutes brainstorming ideas for communicating the results of this workshop to your work teams") to formal ("your workshop packet identifies which breakout group you have been assigned to, the leader and recorder, and the room you'll be meeting in").

How these elements are used in designing a specific workshop is up to you. The rest of this chapter offers guidance on putting a workshop together. But if you are experienced in workshop planning, you may prefer to go directly to the resources (starting on page 143).

Case history: A strategic role for HR

A successful services firm with several thousand professionals nationwide was growing rapidly. The HR department was growing also. With 140 people, and growth expected to continue, the group was beginning to lose its tight-knit sense of identity. Staff members were located throughout the US and Canada. Many didn't know more than a handful of their colleagues on a face-to-face basis.

The group had a primarily administrative role. But the VP for HR, prompted by the CEO's concerns about the quality and depth of the function, believed that this role should become broader and deeper. HR staff members should be business partners and advisers to the teams they worked with. Such relationships had evolved in some regions, based on the skills and experience of those involved. The leaders in those areas appreciated and endorsed the HR staffers' strategic, business-focused role.

But a first attempt to extend this new service model was greeted with indifference by local leaders accustomed to HR's more traditional and limited role. They continued to make people-related decisions without consulting their HR team members, and rarely invited HR to leadership team meetings. As one local leader said, "I'll bring these folks into the business planning process when I know they can contribute. But, let's face it: they're administrators, not business strategists."

The department needed to build a new way of doing business around upgraded skills and capabilities. This would require hiring, training, and re-aligning staff to ensure that the right skills were deployed in the right places.

To launch the planning and transition process, the VP planned a two-day, off-site meeting with all HR staff. A team was assigned to research, plan, and execute the event. They had clear guidance on the expected outcome. They were to reach agreement on the new framework, develop role definitions, create training and development processes, and map out implementation responsibilities and timing. They had discretion to define the process through which they would reach this result.

The team's first action was to conduct a detailed needs assessment through interviews with managers. Next, they gathered input from HR team members through an online survey exploring capabilities, interests, and career goals. They also sought ideas for building a stronger and more customer- and business-focused department.

The workshop process emphasized small breakout sessions with a minimum of time in the full group. Breakout sessions started with an analysis of issues and needs, and moved—during the two days—to the development of detailed recommendations in key areas.

Feedback to participants, including summaries of decisions, questions, and ideas, was provided at the end of the first day. This information was available to guide and focus work on the second day.

Team members handled the facilitation of breakout groups. A half-day, training session (before the meeting) provided guidance, tools, and role-playing practice to team members with little facilitation experience.

Following the workshop, a detailed series of reports confirmed actions and responsibilities.

During the next year, the department grew and changed. Many individuals successfully made the transition to a more advisory and partnership-based role. Some left, unable or unwilling to engage in the new approach.

However, insights and decisions from the workshop helped establish a new direction. The workshop created and sustained a major shift in positioning. Internal customers reported a significant upgrade in the value and effectiveness of the group.

OVERVIEW OF THE MEETING PLANNING PROCESS

Following are suggested steps for building your own workshop. Note that the focus is on the agenda and process, not on logistics (e.g., location, travel arrangements, meals, facilities, meeting rooms).[39]

The steps can be undertaken by a team—and very likely will be for large meetings. But for smaller meetings, they can be handled by an individual. These are the major phases:

- ◆ Create a planning framework
- ◆ Develop the workshop
- ◆ Test and finalize the approach
- ◆ Implement the workshop
- ◆ Follow up and monitor results

---

39. A short meeting-planning checklist is included as Resource 5.4 (page 147).

Create a planning framework
One of the keys to successful change is ensuring that key people and stakeholders are involved and engaged in the process.

Identify a planning team
Forming a small, informal workshop-planning team—probably composed of a representative sample of the expected attendees—can help engage colleagues and others. This team can ensure that the workshop's goals reflect the needs, strategy, and culture of the organization, and that the process and topics reflect the issues and purpose.

Planning team members might include the following:

- The leader and/or sponsor of the change process.
- Members of key stakeholder groups—including those who will benefit, and those who may perceive the changes as negative.
- Managers whose operations will be affected.
- Specialists (e.g., HR staff) with experience and skills that will be helpful in leading or facilitating workshop sessions.

Clarify workshop goals
You want to ensure that the workshop is in alignment with the change process, provides an appropriate and clearly defined platform on which to build the workshop, and enables accurate assessment of the results.

So, the next step is to establish clear goals for the workshop. Review the broad purpose and specific goals set out in Resource 5.3 and modify those to align with the changes that are planned or in process. Seek input from others in finalizing and clarifying these goals—perhaps with a draft set of goals as a basis for discussion. The workshop overview includes a model statement of purpose and goals that can provide you with a starting point.

Identify workshop participants
There is no right number or composition of participants. Generally, your challenge will be to balance the presence of key stakeholders, and the set of skills and functions represented, with practical limitations on the size of the meeting. You will need to avoid taking too many key

people away from their ongoing tasks while still including those with the knowledge, skills, and experience to achieve the workshop goals.

Your planning team represents core stakeholders. Workshop participants are, in effect, an expansion of that team—a broader group who will initiate and drive the change in a positive and effective way. The number and composition of participants needs to reflect the type of change, the anticipated impact, and the communication challenges.

For major change initiatives, there may be a need for several planning and development meetings. A useful model is to start the process with a meeting of core team members, and follow up (once a structure and process have been defined) with a series of further meetings, each focusing on a specific issue related to the change.[40]

Conduct the assessment

You can use e-mail to seek initial input from your team (and others) on issues, goals, topics, and process. See Resource 5.1 (page 143) for an e-mail template. The same e-mail can set the scene for the team's advisory and planning role.

Throughout the change process, it is helpful to maintain a continuing process or cycle of input, assessment, feedback, and action. This helps to develop and strengthen ideas and plans. You can distribute materials to a broader audience if you want to manage expectations, avoid surprises, and seek additional input from senior leaders and others.

Such processes afford a useful reality check. They ensure that you're operating consistently with leaders' intentions and expectations.

Develop the workshop

Establish the elements of the agenda

The agenda/process templates starting on page 149 provide a framework for constructing the workshop agenda. They focus, at varying levels of detail and intensity (based on the workshop format: one day or half-day), on some or all of these core elements:

---

40. For example, follow-up sessions might focus on HR issues, sales and marketing planning, IT, reward systems, facilities planning and development, and other key topics. These sessions would involve people working on those specific issues.

- *Update:* Brief participants on what's happening, why, and what has been decided and planned so far.
- *Information:* Provide an opportunity for participants to express themselves, to "clear the air," and to express concerns. Get everyone on the same page.
- *SWOT analysis:* Identify and assess strengths, weaknesses, opportunities, and threats (or obstacles).
- *Issues:* Build an inventory of issues, questions, and challenges that need to be addressed.
- *Stakeholders:* Determine who will be affected by the change, how they might react, and what their needs for information and support might be.
- *Solutions:* Begin to identify tactics and processes that will effectively address the issues and support achievement of the goals of the change initiative.
- *Planning:* Determine how the change will be managed, who will play what role, what resources will be needed, and how the effort will be driven, supported, coordinated, and assessed.
- *Next steps:* Ensure that all participants are clear about what happens next and who will be doing what, including direct follow-up (e.g., documenting input from breakout groups, communicating with work teams and others not at the workshop).
- *Assessment:* Evaluate how participants feel about the process and how it can be strengthened for future workshops.

Start with one of the agenda templates (Resources 5.5 and 5.6 on pages 149 and 152). Develop it with edits, additions, and deletions to align with your organization's needs and characteristics, and the goals that you've defined for the workshop.

Design to the size of the group

The approach outlined in this chapter can be used for small workshops of 6 to 15 people (a group small enough to sit around a conference table) as well as medium-sized workshops (15 to 50 people) and larger ones (more than 50 people). In the latter two cases—and especially if the workshop lasts for more than half a day—you will almost certainly need to divide into smaller groups for part of the time. This helps ensure that everyone has the opportunity to express opinions, ask questions, and offer ideas. It also enables more tasks to be accomplished, since different groups can work on different issues.

For larger meetings, increasing attention needs to be paid to the logistics of managing a large number of people (e.g., allowing sufficient time at breaks, coordinating breakout group feedback, managing food and refreshments).[41]

Balance structure with flexibility

Plan ahead for the likely need to adjust process and content as the workshop develops. Complex workshops rarely unfold exactly as planned, and you need to be ready to take advantage of opportunities and ideas that develop during the workshop.

Time is invariably short. Some sessions will need to run long so that key questions can be resolved, and that means that other sessions must be cut short.

A typical scenario is that if time is not decisively managed by the facilitator or workshop leader, the agenda steadily falls behind schedule. As a result, sessions planned for late in the day are truncated. A key part of the facilitator's role is to make continuing on-the-spot decisions about how the time is being used and—when necessary—to firmly cut discussion and move on.

Be ready to respect and capture divergent points of view

Design an approach that will encourage and welcome diverse viewpoints. The workshop format provides the opportunity to bring together many of the people who will play key roles in the change process. It also offers a significant challenge: they may have widely varied—and perhaps conflicting—needs, beliefs, issues, and goals. The opportunity to identify, discuss, and understand these points of view is one of the most useful aspects of the workshop process.

It is rare to complete a workshop with a finished plan for change in place. Overall, the workshop may be considered a success if information is gathered, concerns are expressed, and ideas are offered. The participants must feel that their ideas (and those of the people they work with

---

41. Small or medium-sized groups still require careful management, but the overall approach can be somewhat informal. As the group gets larger, the need to actively manage the process increases significantly.

and in a sense represent) will be heard beyond the meeting. Clear processes for capturing information help create this confidence.

Identify leaders/facilitators

Engage people with facilitation skills to lead the overall meeting as well as its components. You should identify someone to act as the overall leader-facilitator for the workshop.

This person probably won't be running breakout sessions, working groups, or other subcomponents of the workshop, but will be responsible for guiding the overall process: keeping the workshop moving and on track; summarizing as necessary; keeping participants involved, informed, and motivated; handling logistical issues including schedule changes; and, above all, monitoring the process and making course corrections as necessary.

The importance of skilled leadership

A skilled and experienced facilitator is a key asset in achieving a successful result. If you don't have the right skills and experience, look for people in your organization who have a successful track record of leading meetings.

As this lengthy list suggests, the leader-facilitator role is an important and challenging one, and experience can be invaluable. If you are not the person to take on the leadership role, look around to find someone in your organization with the right skills, training, and background. In some cases (especially in smaller organizations where these skills may not be available), you may want to look outside the organization for a professional facilitator.

You will probably need other people to act as leaders and/or note-takers in breakout sessions and other components of the workshop. Seek people with relevant experience and skills. In most organizations, you will find people who can do a good job in this role. See Resource 5.9 (page 157) for guidelines on leading breakout sessions.

Plan breakout sessions

Define tasks that are best handled in smaller groups. For meetings with more than 12 to 15 people, you will probably want to break the group into smaller subgroups or breakout sessions for significant periods of time. Breakout can be highly effective in the context of larger meetings:

- They provide a chance for more people to express themselves.
- They increase the number of people who play an active role in the workshop (e.g., by leading the discussions and/or recording and reporting on the input).
- They enable the large group to cover more ground, and work on multiple issues and plans, by the split into smaller sub-groups.
- They offer participants the opportunity to spend part of the day with others with similar interests (e.g., systems design, sales).
- They give the meeting leader(s) a break, and an opportunity to assess progress, adjust the process as needed, and gather input to help guide the rest of the workshop.
- People may offer opinions more openly in a smaller group.
- Above all, people enjoy and respond to the energy and interchange of lively discussion in a small group.

Here are some keys to successful breakout sessions:

- Establish a clearly defined topic and goal, so that time isn't lost as the group struggles to answer the question, "Why are we here?"
- Identify the person responsible for facilitating discussion: keeping it focused, on track, and within time constraints.
- Ensure that someone is responsible for taking notes. This can be the facilitator, but leading the meeting may be easier if that individual is not also focusing on note-taking.
- Provide feedback to breakout session participants and also seek it: invite them to comment on the process.

A significant challenge in using breakout sessions as part of a large-scale meeting is assuring participants that their input will be heard and used. If time permits only a few highlights of feedback to be shared, participants may be concerned that the rest of their ideas will be ignored or lost. And during a fast-moving change process, this is a very real risk. So you need to ensure effective recording and note-taking to stimulate further discussion and guide decision-making.

The output from these breakouts is a valuable resource. It contains information about issues, questions, and concerns that will be shared by employees at large (and/or other stakeholders). It is also a rich source of ideas about how the change can be successfully managed. It can be used in assembling FAQ guides for employees;[42] preparing to address the needs of various stakeholders; and in planning other aspects of the change process.

Accordingly, it's recommended that note-takers for breakout sessions summarize the material in a brief "highlights" report. This may be just a single page of summary points. In a multiday meeting, summaries can be e-mailed to participants with an invitation to respond with any additional insights and/or corrections.

In practice, a relatively small proportion of participants act on this invitation. But even if they take no action, they are now assured that they have been heard and that their input has been noted. They can be confident that the summary will be passed on to those responsible for leading the change.

Providing feedback from breakout sessions to the full group is a notoriously challenging task that can lead to lengthy, unfocused reporting. One effective model is to have the main group facilitator call on each breakout group in turn to share two or three highlights—no more—from their discussion. If later groups find their key points have been covered, they can say so and save time.

> **Share notes with participants**
>
> It can be very helpful to provide participants with notes on breakout sessions and/or the overall meeting. This can reinforce decisions, clarify key points, and encourage continued discussion and attention to the issues.

Establish a process for feedback and follow-up

Be ready to keep the change process moving after the workshop. This ensures that the session is indeed part of continuing planning and implementation, and not a single, isolated event. Participants will be aware that their input has been heard and valued, and that the results are being applied to action.

Plan in advance for what will happen after the workshop. Specifically, you may go back to participants with a summary and report. It is rare that detailed plans are fully formulated by the end of the work-

---

42. See Chapter 6 (starting on page 165) for examples, and also for guidance and resources on developing FAQs.

shop.[43] However, if those responsible for planning have heard ideas and input from many people, then they are in a great position to begin to build that plan. If they take it back to the workshop participants, saying, in effect, "This is based on your input, please help us refine it and move it forward," they should get further excellent input and guidance—and support as the process continues.

See the section on following up and monitoring (page 140) for ideas and guidance about creating meeting notes and action summaries.

Test and finalize the workshop approach

Share the draft approach with your team and other key individuals to validate and strengthen the plans.

Seek feedback

Set the scene by including the workshop goals, so that reviewers can make the connections between the process you've planned and the desired outcomes. Invite feedback and encourage reviewers to offer additional ideas. Include in this review those who will take on a leadership role of some kind (e.g., facilitating a breakout session) in the workshop.

Review the feedback carefully and make appropriate changes to the process. Take special note of suggestions (or requests—for equipment, note-taking resources, or other facilities) from presenters and others with an active role. It's important that leaders-facilitators feel comfortable about the process and the part they will play in it.

Plan the logistics

See Resource 5.4 (page 147) for a checklist of items that will need to be addressed and planned for, including selection of facilities (e.g., hotel rooms), supporting resources (e.g., projectors, sound systems), rooms for breakout sessions, meals and refreshments, handouts or other resources, and travel arrangements. The goal is to create a setting, process, and support system that make participants feel comfortable and ready to focus fully on participating actively and effectively.

---

43. More typically, a somewhat intimidating and unstructured mass of ideas and questions accumulates during the workshop. Now someone has the challenging but critically important task of molding that material into a coherent summary.

Confirm agenda and processes

Behind each agenda item, you need to have the process and content prepared. As well as defining the individual or individuals responsible for leading each session, you should ensure that they have the material they need.

Discussions in breakout sessions—though crucial to engaging people and generating ideas—can also run long and off-topic, especially as these groups are generally led by individuals without special training or experience as facilitators. This can be addressed in part by providing clear guidance on topic, process, and timing. But you must expect that unless guidance is specific and detailed, the output from the group often may not exactly reflect the tasks assigned.

Be clear about who will lead breakout sessions, who will record, and how feedback will be captured and shared.

If the workshop is led by an experienced facilitator, it can be effective to handle these assignments informally—simply ask the group to break into convenient subgroups and self-select facilitators and recorders. Give each

Prepare breakout session leaders
It may be useful to bring breakout session leaders together in advance to ensure that they're ready to carry out their roles.

group clear direction on the goals for the session. With less experienced facilitators (and larger groups), you may want to determine leadership for each group before the breakout session, and ensure that those leaders are prepared for the role.

Distribute agendas, invitations, and other details

You can now assemble the final package—perhaps with one more review by members of the planning team—and distribute materials to those attending the workshop. Ensure that the document provides the necessary guidance both to participants and to leaders-facilitators. If you are conducting a pre-workshop survey (see Resource 5.8 on page 156), the invitation to complete it can be distributed with the agenda.

Implement the workshop

The resources at the end of this chapter (starting on page 143) offer tools, templates, agendas, and other materials relating to conducting the workshop. Here is a compilation of ideas that can help:

Fifteen ideas for a successful workshop

1. If people will be staying overnight before the meeting, arrange an informal buffet-style meal to be available throughout the evening. Encourage people to stop by and meet fellow attendees.

2. If you plan breakout sessions, bring leaders-facilitators together to review the process and share ideas for making it work well. Be sure they know how results will be shared with the larger group (e.g., two or three highlights from each breakout session).

3. Open with a strong, high-interest session led by a presenter or facilitator who can excite and energize the group. The opening sets the scene, establishes expectations, and can go a long way toward building a successful result.

4. Also early on in the workshop, ensure that everyone fully understands the workshop's purpose and process, and how and what participants are expected to contribute.

5. Establish regular process checks: "Let's take a moment to get some feedback. Anyone want to comment on our progress, any ways in which we need to adjust the process, or other observations to help keep us on track?"

6. Adjust the schedule as necessary. For example, break early if the discussion on one issue has wrapped up and the next agenda item is likely to be challenging or lengthy. With boxed lunches, you can combine the break with small-group discussions.

7. The larger the group, the longer the breaks need to be. Just getting people out of a large meeting room can take 5 minutes or more. Breaks will need to be at least 20 minutes in this case. You will likely need one or more people acting as "break police" to encourage people to finish their phone calls and other conversations and move back into the room.

8. Start and finish every session on time. If you don't, you'll find it even more challenging to stay on schedule—and you'll also encourage latecomers after breaks.

9. Encourage people to take the breaks they need, even while discussion continues. It's practical, flexible, and comfortable; and it limits a rush for the doors (and bathrooms) at official breaks.

10. Maintain flexibility—manage time with care, but recognize that is-sues, ideas, and other needs may suggest that you adapt the schedule as you go.[44]

11. Near the end of the workshop, lead a discussion about how to sum-marize the results so that attendees can brief their teams with con-sistency when they get back to the workplace.

12. Note every issue and question—especially the unresolved ones. These will need attention following the session. They also provide a great start for developing an FAQ guide. You may want to assign someone as full-time note-taker.[45]

13. During breaks (or overnight), check in informally with several par-ticipants and group leaders. Ask them how they think the meeting is going, what they like, and what they'd change. Be ready to adjust ac-cordingly.

14. Consider conducting an evaluation of the workshop before it ends. For a small session, facilitate a "plus-delta" discussion.[46] For a larger session, consider brief (10-minute) breakout sessions to assess and report on the meeting. Or see page 163 for a survey-based assess-ment approach.

15. Keep the process alive. Soon after the workshop, distribute notes. Invite further input and comment and be clear about next steps. Build on the engagement you've created.

Follow up and monitor results

Many workshops reach useful conclusions through a positive process, yet ultimately fail because the follow-up falls short. A good workshop can create momentum, build commitment, and develop ideas and plans.

Distribute summaries and next steps

To preserve and sustain gains made at meetings:

---

44. For example, more time may be needed to address a specific issue of concern, thus forc-ing you to take time out of another session. It is generally better to adjust the schedule, and let people know why, than to overrun and risk upsetting people who lose time from their own sessions.

45. The task isn't to keep detailed minutes of all the discussions, but to record key items to be resolved, answered, or applied.

46. Plus-delta (meaning "positive"-"change") is a good approach for an informal assessment. Ask two questions of the group: What went well and what did you like? What could we do better or differently next time? Responses to the first question open up discussion and en-courage constructive responses to the second question.

- Follow up with thanks to participants and (especially) to leaders and facilitators. Ensure that people's efforts are appreciated and fully recognized.
- Compile a summary of recommendations, decisions, and ideas. This would include, for example, brief notes from all the breakout sessions, and next steps determined in the final session.
- Clearly state those next steps, and ensure that the people responsible for action have this material.
- Keep the process moving: monitor actions and progress, and continue to report back.

These steps reinforce decisions and clarify issues. They offer participants an opportunity to provide further input. And they reinforce integration of ideas and plans into the ongoing activities of the organization—including communicating with those who didn't attend the workshop.

Summaries aren't transcripts or formal minutes. They should be brief (the longer the summary, the less likely it will be read). Perhaps in outline format, a summary should cover major points from the workshop, including the following:

- Key issues, new ideas and agreements, and decisions.
- Follow-up action items, including details of who is responsible for what, as well as timing and resource information.
- Matters to be resolved later or elsewhere and any new questions that were raised—perhaps with suggestions on where and how they should be addressed.[47]
- Reports on breakout sessions.

Distribute the summary or summaries to all workshop participants and ask them to get back to you quickly with any comments or clarification they want to add.

Conduct evaluation
If you didn't ask participants for feedback during the workshop, you should do so soon after it ends. For small workshops you can send an e-

---

47. The list of such items is sometimes referred to as the "parking lot": the place where you park ideas and issues that are important but not directly relevant to the current discussion.

mail asking the plus-delta questions (What worked well and what did you like? What changes would you make?). For larger ones you can distribute a survey.

Online surveys are fast and effective and several services offer low- or no-cost resources for online research. See Resource 2.7 (page 59) for a list. They are easy to use and provide a powerful, fast, and effective way of gathering data. See also Resource 5.12 (page 163) for a simple questionnaire that you can adapt for your own use.

A good practice for motivating action and follow-up is to include in the summary (or in a later follow-up memo or meeting) some recognition for completed action items. Extend a "thank you" to individuals who played major roles in resolving an issue or meeting a goal.

RESOURCE 5.1: SAMPLE E-MAIL FOR SEEKING INPUT

The purpose of this e-mail is to engage the support of a group of advisers, and to gather their input on workshop goals. Adapt this to your needs and send it to members of your planning team and others whose input might be useful.

Subject: Gathering input on workshop goals

On *[date]* we will be holding a planning workshop to confirm the goals for the *[name of initiative]*, identify key issues and obstacles, review stakeholder concerns and needs, evaluate resources, and lay out plans for moving ahead.

I'll be forming a small team or advisory group to guide and assist in planning the workshop and I'd like you to join that team. More details about that will follow. Meanwhile, it will be very helpful if you would think about the questions below and get back to me (via e-mail, by phone, or in person) by *[time]* on *[date]* with brief responses. Many thanks in advance.

- ◆ What do you see as the one or two most important challenges for our organization as we move ahead with *[name of initiative]*?
- ◆ Please list two or three goals that the workshop should aim to achieve.
- ◆ Do you have any suggestions for additional individuals who might make great contributions to the process and who should be invited to the workshop?
- ◆ What ideas do you have about the workshop content, process, and duration?
- ◆ Would you be willing to act as facilitator and/or note-taker for one or more breakout sessions?

Soon after I receive your input, I'll send you a summary of the planned workshop process and a scheduling request for an initial team meeting. Meanwhile, please feel free to send me any immediate comments, questions, or ideas.

RESOURCE 5.2: SAMPLE E-MAIL FOR SEEKING FEEDBACK

The purpose of this e-mail is gather feedback on your workshop design.

Subject: Seeking feedback on initial ideas

Many thanks for your responses to my e-mail about workshop planning.

Attached is the agenda and overall design for the Change Planning Workshop scheduled for *[date]* at *[location]*. It reflects the feedback you provided. Your perceptions and ideas have greatly influenced the way this is coming together. I believe we're on the way to developing a workshop that will make a real contribution to our planning.

[Add comments on the workshop design—see example below.]

You'll see that the process includes significant time for work in small groups, during which we will aim to develop ideas for an effective, timely, and focused implementation plan. When we get to a more detailed draft, you'll see that a number of you are identified to lead or otherwise contribute to several of the sessions. Nearer the time of the workshop, we'll have some specific discussions with these "faculty" members to ensure that everyone fully understands—and is prepared for—their roles in the workshop.

Please review the agenda and the approach and get back to me with any feedback by *[date]*. Again, thanks for helping shape the process.

RESOURCE 5.3: SAMPLE E-MAIL WITH WORKSHOP OVERVIEW

An e-mail based on the template below can provide an overview of your workshop's purpose and approach. It can also invite and encourage feedback. Send it to members of your team and others who will have useful input and/or significant roles in the workshop.

To: Workshop planning team

As we start to build an organization-wide plan to implement the *[initiative name]*, we will be holding a planning workshop to gather input, identify issues and challenges, and begin to develop plans. We appreciate your comments, questions and ideas about this process.

Specific goals

- ◆ Bring the participants up to date on the business case for change, work done to date, and their roles in the process.
- ◆ Determine ways to gather input from all parts of the organization on the issues, challenges, and needs to address as we implement the change.
- ◆ Assess impact on key stakeholders, including customers, employees, suppliers, stockholders, business partners, and others.
- ◆ Begin to identify the key actions and steps needed to ensure the success of the change, and how these will be assigned, managed, resourced, and timed.
- ◆ Gain the group's buy-in on next steps, roles, and responsibilities.

Expected outcomes

- ◆ Clear, shared understanding of issues and challenges that we will be addressing, based on an open and lively exchange of ideas.
- ◆ Increased sense of teamwork and confidence in *[organization name]*'s ability to establish targets and develop plans.
- ◆ An inventory of issues, questions, and ideas to draw on as we continue to implement the change.

RESOURCE 5.3 [CONTINUED]

Pre-workshop process

- Workshop participants will complete a brief online questionnaire, including SWOT analysis (strengths, weaknesses, opportunities, threats) and key priorities.
- Questionnaire data will be summarized and presented during the workshop to focus the group on key issues and opportunities.
- All participants will be encouraged to engage their teams in discussions of the issues, so they come equipped with input and insights from a cross section of the people they work with.

Workshop agenda

- See Resources 5.5 and 5.6 (pages 149 and 152) for one-day and half-day agendas.

Post-workshop process

- Workshop output will be edited and compiled into a report for reference and follow-up. Participants will have a chance to review this before it is finalized.
- The team planning the change will draw on results as they confirm priorities and actions, develop plans and processes, and establish monitoring and follow-up.
- Workshop participants will also discuss results with their teams, and will work with their teams as they continue to address issues identified at the workshop.

RESOURCE 5.4: CHECKLIST ON WORKSHOP PLANNING

Start planning the logistics of the workshop by reviewing this checklist and making notes of ideas, tasks, and responsibilities.

Elements to consider in planning a workshop

Workshop title

Date(s)

Location

Purpose

Sponsor(s)

Planning team role and responsibilities

Planning team members

Communication needs (e.g., with managers of those attending)

Workshop budget

Cost recording and management

Number of attendees

Organizational roles of attendees

Selection/identification criteria and process

Responsibilities at the workshop

List or database of attendees

Timing of invitations and acceptances

Others to be notified (e.g., managers of attendees)

Speakers and facilitators

RESOURCE 5.4 [CONTINUED]

External resources

Travel and accommodations

Expense handling

Presentation materials (e.g., PowerPoint, other visuals, handouts)

Communication with participants (timing, responsibility, resources)

Handouts and/or packet of meeting materials (including agenda)

Meeting rooms—main and breakout

Meals and refreshments

Transportation

Equipment (e.g., screens, projectors, flip charts, notepads, pens, pointers, audio and audiovisual equipment)

Electronic and other communications (e.g., phones, network access, delivery services, fax, message handling)

Follow-up

Workshop summary

Evaluation

Decisions and next steps

Communication with those not at the workshop

[Other]

[Other]

RESOURCE 5.5: TEMPLATE FOR A ONE-DAY WORKSHOP

This template provides a starting point for your own agenda. Adjust it to reflect the purpose and context. It provides a full day (8:00–5:00) that will call for firm leadership[48] to keep on time and on task—especially with a large group. Three breakout sessions provide opportunities for small-group work and creative problem-solving.

Topic	Timing	Content/process
Workshop introduction	8:00–8:15	Welcome participants; outline the process; review timing and expected outcomes.
Keynote	8:15–9:00	*Update on issues and planned changes* Review status and issues in the organization. Discuss the case for change and progress so far. Report on the pre-workshop survey. Put the workshop in context—expectations, why it's important, what it needs to achieve. Clarify goals for the change in the context of business mission, goals, and values.
Questions and discussion	9:00–9:45	Encourage the group (or breakout groups) to ask questions, discuss key issues, and offer reactions, challenges, and ideas.
Break	9:45–10:00	
Breakout session 1	10:00–11:00	Breakout groups convene. *Outline of the process: Identifying the challenges* Identify key challenges (issues and opportunities), starting with those identified in the pre-workshop questionnaire (if conducted). Group the challenges into broad headings or categories (e.g., people, customers, costs, systems). Identify the two or three highest-priority issues within each category. (More details of the purpose and process for this session will be provided to breakout leaders.)

---

48. You may want to add a column headed "Session leader".

RESOURCE 5.5 [CONTINUED]

Topic	Timing	Content/process
Share highlights	11:00–11:30	Full group reconvenes. Breakout session leaders outline discussion highlights and illustrate key issues and ideas.
Stakeholder assessment	11:30–12:00	Presenter outlines major stakeholder groups (i.e., those who will most influence and/or be influenced by the outcome of the change).[49]
Breakout session 2 (lunch session; boxed lunches provided)	12:00–1:00	Breakout groups reconvene with boxed lunches. *Outline of the process: Problem-solving and planning* Review the major issues identified in the first breakout sessions and shared with the full group. Brainstorm possible actions and processes to address the key issues and needs. Identify the one or two highest-priority actions or tactics in each category. Prepare a summary to share with the full group. (More details of the purpose and process for this session will be provided to breakout leaders.)
Share highlights	1:00–1:30	Full group reconvenes. Breakout session leaders outline discussion highlights and illustrate key issues and ideas.
Breakout preparation	1:30–1:45	Review open issues and questions and allocate topics (e.g., career impact, technology, training, reward systems) to breakout groups.

49. Examples include employees, customers, directors, stockholders, managers, supervisors, media, government, communities, labor unions, competitors, suppliers, partners, and many others.

RESOURCE 5.5 [CONTINUED]

Topic	Timing	Content/process
Breakout session 3	1:45–3:00	Breakout groups reconvene.
		Outline of the process: Defining questions and answers
		Groups produce output of 10–12 high-priority questions within the topic area, together with concise and direct answers.
		Senior leaders and/or functional experts move from group to group to act as expert resources and guide development of responses.
		Some questions will be unanswered; pass them on for further work by other individuals or teams.
		(More details of the purpose and process for this session will be provided to breakout leaders before the workshop.)
Break	3:00–3:15	
Report	3:15–3:45	Full group reconvenes.
		Breakout leaders report results to the full group.
Open session (panel discussion)	3:45–4:30	*Outline of the process: Putting it together*
		Panel of leaders reviews the input, focusing on identification of next steps and summarizing recommended action.
		Open the session to questions and discussion.
		Discuss how and when to communicate workshop results with workgroups and others.
Assessment	4:30–4:45	Review workshop process and results.
		Use a plus-delta assessment: what worked well; what could be changed.[50]
Workshop close	4:45–5:00	Close with thanks to participants, and comments from the workshop facilitator and a senior leader/sponsor.

---

50. In the plus-delta assessment approach, the facilitator asks two questions of the group: What went well and what did you like? What could we do better or differently next time? Responses to the first question open up discussion and encourage people to offer constructive input to the second.

RESOURCE 5.6: TEMPLATE FOR A HALF-DAY WORKSHOP

This template provides a starting point for constructing your own workshop agenda. Adjust it to reflect the purpose and context of the workshop. It provides a very full half day (8:00–12:30) and includes two breakout sessions. To cover the required ground, the process needs to move fast and calls for a skilled meeting leader to keep sessions on track.[51] A fast pace and challenging time constraint can generate a sense of excitement and energy, and focus attention on the task.

Topic	Timing	Content/process
Workshop introduction	8:00–8:10	Welcome participants; outline the process; review timing and expected outcomes.
Keynote	8:10–8:45	*Update on issues and planned changes*
		Review status and issues in the business.
		Discuss the case for change and outline progress so far.
		Identify the behavior you want to change and address how supporting systems will be aligned with these new expectations.
		Review plans for next steps.
		Put the workshop in context—expectations, why it's important, what it needs to achieve.
		Clarify goals for the change in the context of business mission, goals, and values.
Questions and discussion	8:45–9:20	Encourage the group (or groups)[52] to ask questions and raise issues of interest and concern.
		Document the input, but focus on listening and discussion.
Break	9:20–9:30	

---

51. You may want to insert an additional column headed "Session leader."
52. If the numbers are large, this can be handled by breaking up into informal groups without leaving the meeting room. Each group discusses questions and issues and then identifies the two or three of highest priority. After 15–20 minutes, the facilitator polls each group in turn. In this way most high-priority and high-concern issues and questions can be raised without the time-consuming need to move to separate rooms, get a discussion moving, conclude it, and return.

RESOURCE 5.6 [CONTINUED]

Topic	Timing	Content/process
Breakout session 1	9:30–10:15	Breakout groups convene. *Outline of the process: Identifying the challenges* Identify key challenges (issues and opportunities), starting with those identified in the pre-workshop questionnaire (if conducted). Group challenges into broad headings or categories (e.g., people, resources, customers, costs, systems). Identify the two or three highest-priority issues within each category. (More details of the purpose and process for this session will be provided to breakout leaders.)
Share high-lights	10:15–10:35	Full group reconvenes. Breakout session leaders outline discussion highlights and illustrate key issues and ideas. Facilitator clarifies and summarizes the issues in each heading or category.
Breakout session 2	10:35–11:15	Breakout groups reconvene. *Outline of the process: Problem-solving and planning* Review major issues identified in the first breakout sessions and shared with the full group. Brainstorm possible actions and processes to address these. Identify the one or two highest-priority actions or tactics in each category. Prepare a summary. (More details of the purpose and process for this session will be provided to breakout leaders.)
Share high-lights	11:15–11:35	Full group reconvenes. Breakout session leaders outline discussion highlights and illustrate key issues and ideas.

RESOURCE 5.6 [CONTINUED]

Topic	Timing	Content/process
Break	11:35–11:45	
Open session (panel discussion)	11:45–12:20	*Outline of the process: Putting it together* Panel of senior leaders reviews and discusses input and ideas, focusing on identification of next steps (primarily compiling input and summarizing recommended actions). Open up to questions and discussion. Discuss as a group how and when to communicate workshop results with workgroups and other teams and individuals.
Assessment and close	12:20–12:30	Review workshop process and results. Use a plus-delta assessment: what worked well; what could be changed. Close with thanks to participants and comments from the workshop facilitator and a senior leader/sponsor.

RESOURCE 5.7: SAMPLE E-MAIL TO WORKSHOP PARTICIPANTS

This sample e-mail text can be used to invite participants to the workshop, set their expectations, and ask them to complete the pre-workshop questionnaire (if one is planned). The e-mail might also be sent for information purposes to managers of those attending the workshop.

Subject: Invitation to the change planning workshop

This confirms that we are looking forward to seeing you on *[date]* at the *[name of workshop]*. The session starts at 8:00 a.m.; a continental breakfast will be available from 7:15 a.m. We'll wrap up at 5:00 p.m.

The broad purpose of the workshop is to start building an organization-wide plan to implement the *[name of change initiative]*.

Specific goals include the following:

- Bring the *[name of team or group]* up to date on the business case for change, and the work that has been done so far.
- Gather input from all parts of the organization on the issues and challenges to be addressed as we implement the change.
- Assess the impact on key stakeholders, including customers, employees, and business partners.
- Begin to identify the key actions we need to take, and how these will be managed, resourced, and timed.
- Agree on next steps and the role of the *[name of team or group]*.

We also want to gather input and ideas from people who won't be attending the workshop. So please talk with your teams before and after we meet. Keep them updated, seek their input, and discuss with them the actions and solutions that will support our continued success.

[Include the following paragraph if you are conducting a pre-workshop survey.]

To help us prepare, we would like you to complete a brief questionnaire about strengths, weaknesses, opportunities, threats, and key actions or projects that we need to invest in. You will find the questionnaire at *[URL]*. It shouldn't take more than a few minutes to complete.

Please come ready to participate fully and to offer your ideas. You will be helping us build plans to ensure the success of *[name of change initiative]* and to guide our continued growth.

We're looking forward to seeing you on *[date]*. Meanwhile, please let me know if you have any immediate comments or questions.

RESOURCE 5.8: SAMPLE GUIDE TO PRE-WORKSHOP SURVEY

This resource provides a questionnaire template you can adapt for a pre-workshop survey. Gathering input ahead of the workshop helps to ensure a focused and successful event. You'll have a better understanding of the expectations of those attending; you'll get information to help build the agenda; and you'll be aware of key questions and issues.

You can approach this informally, by holding in-person or telephone conversations with a few people; you can conduct a somewhat more formal survey by sending an e-mail with a few questions; or you can develop broad input via an online survey. Many organizations have internal resources that are able to handle a survey such as this. If you don't have such resources, you can use one of several web-based services that support simple surveys at no charge (see page 56 for a list).

Subject: Pre-workshop survey

Please take a few minutes to respond to these questions. A summary will be presented during the *[name of workshop]*. This will help us focus our energies on issues and ideas that are of the greatest importance.

By all means, discuss the questions with your team as you consider your answers. And please help us by keeping your comments very concise: just two or three points under each heading. You'll have plenty of opportunities at the meeting to discuss your ideas at greater length!

Your input is anonymous: no data will be associated with specific individuals. Many thanks for your help.

Suggested survey content

Strengths: As we prepare to implement *[name of change initiative]*, what are some of *[organization name]*'s greatest strengths?

Weaknesses: Identify areas where we may be vulnerable or where major change or improvement is needed.

Opportunities: What improvement and growth opportunities do you see that we should pursue?

Threats: What could challenge our success? Do you see threats from competitors, changing technology, or other sources?

Questions: What are the most important questions that occur to you and/or your team as we prepare to move ahead with the change?

Ideas: What actions or initiatives could strongly support the change?

Other: Please add any other observations, ideas, and topics that you would like to be discussed at the workshop.

RESOURCE 5.9: GUIDELINES FOR BREAKOUT SESSION LEADERS

Develop notes and guidance for breakout session leaders using these guidelines and the facilitation tactics in Resources 5.10 and 5.11 (pages 159 and 161).

Purpose of session

Identify key challenges (issues and opportunities) that need to be addressed as we implement the change. A later breakout session will develop ideas, tactics, and solutions.

Leader's role

Keep the discussion focused; manage time; limit discussion if necessary to move on; encourage contributions from all present; ensure that everyone has an opportunity to offer input and ideas; and maintain energy, focus, and respectful interaction.

Note-taker's role

Take notes of key points (it need not be a full transcript), especially of areas of strong agreement. Please also record questions that the group raises but does not or cannot answer, for later review and response.

Toward the end of the session, share your summary and ensure that you have a consensus on what will be shared with the larger group.

If the workshop is longer than one day, e-mail a concise summary of the session to all breakout group participants. Invite them to comment, and add or amend as needed, before the notes are passed on to the person who is coordinating the overall meeting. This will help to ensure that all input is captured and retained whether or not it is shared at the feedback session following the breakout session.

Time management (suggested schedule)

Here are guidelines on how to use the available 45 minutes:

- *15 minutes:* Brainstorm issues, questions, obstacles, ideas.
- *15 minutes:* Organize and clarify the responses; eliminate redundancies; group the issues under appropriate categories (e.g., people, resources, customers, costs, systems).
- *10 minutes:* Identify the top two or three issues in each category.
- *5 minutes:* Review unanswered questions and identify the two or three that the group most wants to hear addressed.

RESOURCE 5.9 [CONTINUED]

Opening talking points (examples)

"We'll start by taking 10 or 15 minutes to brainstorm issues and questions about the change."

"We'll get everything summarized on flip charts as we go—try to be concise and help out our recorder here."

"Everything is on the table: ask questions, voice concerns, and offer your ideas. Later, we'll organize, clarify, and prioritize all the results so we can go back to the full group with a few clear and useful highlights."

"The next breakout session will move a step further, developing tactics, answers, and solutions."

"So let's get started. What's on your mind about the changes? What are the issues and questions?"

RESOURCE 5.10: KEEPING BREAKOUT SESSIONS ON TRACK

As a breakout session develops, some participants may display negative or unhelpful behaviors. You could include the tactics here in your guidance to session leaders.

As the meeting develops, participants will display a wide range of behaviors, positive and negative. Positive behaviors include speaking concisely and clearly, helping to summarize complex points, introducing ideas that move the discussion forward, providing positive feedback to others, and injecting humor when appropriate.

Negative behaviors include introducing digressions, focusing on personal issues at the expense of the shared task, maintaining opposing opinions without offering suggestions, displaying negative body language or attitudes without expressing the nature of the problem, and (a frequent challenge) making lengthy and sometimes irrelevant contributions that slow the process down.

Here are a few tactics for dealing with each.

Introducing digressions

"This is an important issue and I appreciate that you've raised it—but I think we might all agree that dealing with [topic] should be our main focus."

"I'd like to put this on the list of other subjects that we need to address, and make sure that today we stay focused on [topic]."

Focusing on personal issues

"I understand your concern about this, but it seems that it's more a personal issue that you need to address with your supervisor—it's not within the scope of what we're here to do."

Objecting or resisting without offering positive suggestions

"It's good that we're hearing every point of view here, but it seems to me that you've been focusing on reasons these proposals won't work, rather than looking for ideas that might work—or ways of making the existing approach more effective. Can you give us some ideas about how you'd address the issue?"

RESOURCE 5.10 [CONTINUED]

Displaying negative body language or attitude

You may choose to address this privately—in a break—or you may decide to deal with it head-on.

"You seem uncomfortable with some aspects of the discussion—I've noticed that you're frowning and shaking your head in a way that suggests that you don't like the way this is going. But you haven't made a comment for a while. Is there something troubling you that you'd like to share with us?"

Making lengthy contributions that slow the process down

"Sorry to step in here, but we've got limited time and need to move along. We must make sure everyone has the opportunity to contribute."

RESOURCE 5.11: REVIEW AND CLOSURE OF BREAKOUTS

Check progress as you go; summarize, clarify, and evaluate. These notes suggest tactics for assessing how the breakout session is going—and doing so in time to make adjustments as indicated.

Mid-meeting checklist

A checklist helps you assess for yourself how the process is going without interrupting the flow of the discussion.

- Are you getting input from everyone?
- Has someone with important knowledge or experience not contributed much?
- Is the time being used effectively—are you making progress?
- Are you staying pretty much on topic, without many digressions?
- Have new issues arisen that need to be addressed?
- Are you keeping track of what has been set aside for now but that will need later follow-up?
- How do the participants feel about the progress of the session?

You may want to put at least the final issue to the group:

"Can we spend a minute reflecting on whether we're on track? How do you feel about the process, and our progress? Is there anything we should be doing differently?"

Closure

Before the time set for the discussion to end, suggest that the group spend a few minutes summarizing progress, clarifying conclusions, and discussing next steps.

These will include defining who should be doing what and when (e.g., how feedback to the full group will be handled). At the least, you should summarize the major points and validate them with particpants.

End the session on time, and be sure to thank everyone for their contributions.

RESOURCE 5.11 [CONTINUED]

Feedback

Participants in a well-run session appreciate being part of a process in which distractions and digressions are limited, the group is kept on task, time is managed well, and there is a clear set of outcomes.

Seek feedback by asking two simple questions:

- What went well—what did you like about this session?
- What would you change to improve the process next time?

These questions constitute the plus-delta assessment process. The first question encourages a positive frame of mind and reinforces what worked well. The second gives people an opportunity to offer constructive criticism and ideas for improvement.

You can use plus-delta during a couple of minutes of informal conversation—gather a few quick comments in each category. Or you can take a slightly more formal (and more time-consuming) approach, writing comments on flip charts and engaging the group in some discussion, especially around the areas for improvement, and perhaps reaching agreement on what will be done differently next time.

Be sure to include a summary of this input in your follow-up notes.

RESOURCE 5.12: TEMPLATE FOR WORKSHOP ASSESSMENT

This template is an effective online questionnaire, but can also be administered on paper.[53] For a small group, you could perform an informal assessment and send a few key questions via e-mail.

Please give us your feedback on the workshop.

Your assessment and ideas will guide us as we plan future sessions.
1 = very good; 2 = good; 3 = neutral/no opinion; 4 = poor; 5 = very poor.

What is your overall assessment of the workshop?	1 2 3 4 5
How do you rate the breakout sessions you attended?	
[Name of session]	1 2 3 4 5
[Name of session]	1 2 3 4 5

Please assess these elements

Meeting rooms and facilities	1 2 3 4 5
Meals and refreshments	1 2 3 4 5
Travel arrangements	1 2 3 4 5
Workshop leadership and facilitation	1 2 3 4 5
Use of time	1 2 3 4 5
Advance notice and pre-meeting activity	1 2 3 4 5
Follow-up report	1 2 3 4 5

What two or three aspects did you like best, or feel worked well?

What would you change or do differently?

What was the most positive outcome of the workshop for you?

Are there any issues or challenges that you feel were left unresolved?

Please add any further comments and ideas below.

Many thanks for your input!

---

53. If this survey is administered online, respondents will probably be checking a box. If it's used on paper, they might circle a number.

CHAPTER 6

Developing FAQ guides

IDENTIFY AND ADDRESS QUESTIONS IN ADVANCE

Change raises questions and concerns, presents operational challenges, and imposes demands on time and resources. The cost of managing the process is greatly increased if attention is diverted from day-to-day operations.

We often see significant changes implemented with scant attention to identifying and addressing the challenges it may create among those involved, the questions it will raise, and the issues and needs it will generate. A variety of tools and processes can address these needs and greatly enhance the quality and effectiveness of the process. One such tool is a familiar but underutilized one: a comprehensive set of questions and answers collected in what's often called a Frequently Asked Questions (FAQ) document.

An effective FAQ supports the core factors in effective change in several ways. When deployed, it has a clear role in communication: it will assist stakeholders—those involved and affected, including employees, managers, and customers—by providing a wide variety of information about the change. The FAQ development process also builds engagement and support; and identifies possible sources of resistance, and the reasons. It's a useful tool for managers as they deal with employee questions and concerns.

By identifying challenging questions, and assembling the answers, a development process that deeply involves key stakeholder groups can also help drive the change planning effort. Each question implies an issue that needs to be recognized and addressed.

CREATING THE FAQ DOCUMENT: PROCESS OVERVIEW

This chapter outlines a team process for creating a strong FAQ document. This can range from a short e-mail with responses to a few key questions, to a comprehensive online resource that's regularly updated and enables user-added questions, issues, and ideas. The development approach and tools in this chapter can be used to build a document that falls anywhere on that spectrum.

Ideally, you will have been tracking questions and issues throughout the change planning process (e.g., issues that arose during meetings with stakeholder groups affected by the change). If so, you may already have a good foundation for building the FAQ document.

The suggested process has four major phases. In the pages immediately following the summary below, you will find details and suggestions for each phase. Among the resources starting on page 176 you'll find tools and templates, as well as a variety of standard questions and responses that are ready for you to adapt and use.

Phase 1: Form a team

Build a group of key contributors. Look for people who are well-informed about the change, people involved in it, and people able to offer input on likely issues and concerns.

A planning tool

Identifying key questions and preparing responses provides a resource that can drive management action to support change. For example, questions about systems support can trigger action to ensure that IT systems are aligned with the new direction.

Phase 2: Identify questions and issues

Use brainstorming or another process to identify questions and issues, and then organize them into categories. For more complex and extensive changes, conduct an assessment among stakeholders.

Phase 3: Develop responses

Develop responses, or seek additional guidance where these aren't available. Review the material as necessary with organizational leaders. Edit for clarity, brevity, and consistency.

Phase 4: Test and deploy the guide

Test the draft by inviting representative stakeholders to read it and comment. Incorporate changes and upgrades, and then distribute and promote the FAQ guide. Use it to encourage additional input, promote consistent communication, and build support for the change.

PHASE 1: FORM A TEAM

A team can bring very helpful perspectives and roles to the process. Engage people who represent or are familiar with the stakeholders who are affected by the changes. This will help to ensure that your FAQ guide reflects stakeholders' issues and concerns. (If you're working on your own, go to phase 2.)

Whether the change is organization-wide or on a local scale, you want to engage the right people for your team. This includes those who have a good understanding of the employee groups (or other stakeholders) most affected by the changes. Members might include the following:

> **Take advantage of other processes**
> In the early planning phases of a change effort, monitor meetings, e-mail, and other interactions. Note questions about rationale, expected impact, process, and other topics. These questions can form the basis for your FAQ and also guide planning and development work.

- Leaders responsible for planning the change.
- Employees involved and affected, and/or managers and supervisors who will be aware of employee ideas and concerns.
- HR representatives who work closely with these employees.
- Sales team leaders who are familiar with the needs of customers, partners, and suppliers.
- Specialists with expertise that will enhance the input and process (e.g., a strong writer-editor).
- External-relations and/or marketing staff who are familiar with media and with industry and competitor groups.

In times of organizational change, many of the people involved will have questions, concerns, and ideas of their own. Most will welcome a chance to be heard. They might be glad to participate in a team that aims to capture the important questions and define how they're addressed.

PHASE 2: IDENTIFY QUESTIONS AND ISSUES

If you've been recording questions and issues throughout the change planning process, you can use them as the foundation for your FAQ guide.[54] If you're starting from scratch, you can use a variety of approaches to identify the issues most likely to be of concern to the people involved in the change.

Use a brainstorming meeting

To launch the process, gather the team in a face-to-face meeting or phone conference. In addition to outlining the goals and process for developing the FAQ guide, this initial meeting gives everyone the chance to see who's involved and how each person can contribute.

> **Try brainstorming tools**
> MindManager includes a brainstorming module.[55] This enables you to record ideas, add categories, and visually map the ideas to those categories. It also offers a variety of simple tools for collaboration and distribution.

Set the tone by sharing an agenda ahead of the meeting and establishing a clear timeline. Many change events evolve fast, with limited time for careful planning. Where time is short, you can accomplish a great deal in one well-managed meeting.

Focus intensely on the end result: anticipating the likely reactions of employees and other stakeholders, and developing concise responses. A small group can identify literally hundreds of questions in an hour or two, especially if it works in two or more smaller groups with each focusing on a specific audience or set of topics.

After organizing and clarifying the material, another few hours can see development of at least a partial set of responses. Below is a suggested process for a meeting in which you assemble an initial draft FAQ. You can use the headings as an agenda.

A process such as this might occupy a full day. It can yield a large volume of data that can inform planning for the change as well as providing the material for building the FAQ document.

---

54. An issue may not be stated as a question, but probably implies one. For example, "If the sales force is going to be offering so many more product alternatives, they're going to need more training and better support material". This can readily be restated as a question and answer: "How can we be equipped to deal with so many new products . . ."
55. A software program from Mindjet (www.mindjet.com).

Provide a welcome and overview
- Explain the purpose of the meeting and ask all participants to introduce themselves (if they don't already know each other).
- Outline the steps for the process the team will take to develop the FAQ guide.
- Discuss any administrative or process questions and issues.

Identify questions
- Ask participants to contribute any questions they've already compiled in the course of planning meetings.
- Ask the group to brainstorm about the issues and needs of specific stakeholders, generating as many questions as they can.
- Record all questions separately (on sticky notes, flip charts, or computer).

Organize questions into categories
- Review the questions and group them into categories, such as business impact, job transitions, career opportunities, severance provisions, relocation issues, training, and others.
- Use an "all other" category for questions that you can't readily classify; as questions accumulate, new categories will emerge.

Edit for clarity and brevity
- Refine questions to be concise and consistent.
- Edit them for clarity—one question for each distinct topic.

Agree on the next steps
- Clearly define responsibilities for developing answers, completing an initial draft, reviewing and editing the material, distributing the FAQ guide, and managing ongoing updates.
- Establish timing and review dates, including future meetings.
- Seek sources of additional guidance and advice for unanswered questions; assign responsibility for gathering input.

Case history: Issue-driven planning

A large health care organization planned to introduce a new compensation system. Pay was going to be linked more closely to market rates, with less emphasis on internal equity. Incentives would be introduced. Benefits were to be adjusted to market levels—some up, some down. The defined-benefit retirement program was going to be replaced by a money purchase (defined-contribution) plan.

The goals were to align better with the market, manage costs more effectively, and provide rewards more closely linked to performance. But the complex interaction of the many different functions, roles, and levels within the organization made it impossible to generalize about the impact of the changes. The reality was that it was a gain for some, a loss for others, and for many a breakeven. The linkage to performance made generalizations even harder—and perhaps misleading.

A cross-organizational team was assembled to implement the changes. Comprising 15 people, the team represented all major functions in the organization. Several members had been part of the design team. They acknowledged the challenge of implementation but offered little guidance about how to accomplish it effectively.

Some focus group research had been conducted by the design team, but there was no data about potential reactions to the final plan. With limited time available, the implementation team decided to start their process with a daylong issue-identification meeting, organized using the afternoon of one day and the morning of the next. This allowed for results to be documented overnight and available at the second part of the meeting.

The team broke into groups of three or four people. Groups changed composition after two hours. They spent the afternoon asking questions, offering ideas, raising issues, arguing, challenging, and evaluating. Each group took detailed notes of every issue, question, and idea. Where answers were available or offered (or guessed) they were recorded as well. Where answers couldn't be provided or developed, the questions were noted and the process moved on.

Overnight, the material was organized into an Excel spreadsheet organized by topic. Some of these were subject-related (e.g., health care, goals and metrics, market-based pay, promotion systems, performance management). Others were process-based (e.g., support for managers, communication, employee involvement, external communication). Duplicates were eliminated, language was clarified, and questions and statements were summarized or abridged.

At the start of the second day, the groups received copies of the spreadsheet with the challenge of identifying the 5 to 10 most important issues and questions under each of the 12 categories. This process forced significant focus. The participants merged similar questions and discarded irrelevant ones.

During a break, results were consolidated into 15 categories (3 new categories emerged from the "all other" catchall category) of 5 to 20 questions. Then the small groups met again. This time the challenge was to formulate or clarify responses. These included not just concise answers to factual questions, but also policy or program ideas to address critical planning issues.

The session yielded a rich database of information. This formed the basis of a detailed FAQ guide, with a version for managers. At least as important, the database provided the framework for implementation planning.

Identify and define the questions

You may complete the initial question-identification process in one meeting, or you may need further assessments. You will probably seek additional input as you formulate responses to some of the questions.

To increase certainty that you're generating the right questions, consider surveying stakeholders (e.g., employees, managers, sales reps) to identify questions and issues. You can do this through informal meetings, focus groups, e-mail or online surveys, or other methods.

Whatever the approach or scale of the effort, you can expect that many of the questions will fall into one of these broad categories:

- *The basic facts about the change:* What's happening? When does it start? Who's in charge? Which groups are affected?
- *The purpose and rationale:* Why are we doing this? What are we trying to achieve? Haven't we tried it before?
- *What individuals and teams need to do:* What do I/we need to do differently? What do I/we have to learn? Who can help? How can I/we contribute?
- *How it will affect the stakeholder concerned:* What happens to me? What's in it for me? Who will I be working with? How will it affect my pay and career?

Using Web 2.0 and social media

Web 2.0 is a descriptor for the "new Internet": more collaborative, interactive, and user-focused systems. This is a significant evolution from Web 1.0—primarily a one-way tool used for distributing information.

The new model is focused on the needs and interests of the users. Interaction and peer-to-peer give and take is what people clearly seek. The result is also useful for collaboration, including online meetings, document review, and real-time commentary and updates.

Social media and networks are a leading part of this trend, and are increasingly becoming not just accepted but also deployed within organizations. Wikis, Twitter, Yammer, blogs, LinkedIn, Facebook, webcasts, and podcasts—all these and many others are finding applications that, when effectively used and managed, can provide businesses with a rich source of information and ideas. They can also stimulate and sustain constructive discussion and collaboration.

At the core of Web 2.0 in business is a major transition in the way information is developed and distributed. In effect, employees at all levels find themselves empowered to share information, issues, concerns, and ideas with all others.

The risk is that not all the information distributed in this way is accurate. But nor was the grapevine or rumor-mill in pre-Internet days. The challenge is to interpret and moderate the flow of information, ideas and opinions, correcting inaccuracies and reinforcing needed messages. Leaders have the opportunity to be far better informed, and in a more timely way, than ever before about what is really happening—and what people are thinking and feeling. And leaders can reach their audiences in a variety of fast, appealing, and effective ways.

Social media make possible conversations and discussions that are an important part of the process of adaptation. These have often been absent from traditional approaches to communication around change.

Organize the information

After brainstorming and/or research, you should have a significant inventory of questions (certainly dozens, probably more than a hundred) covering a wide range of topics. Organizing these into categories helps to refine the issues into clear, concise questions; to consider the implications of each; and to develop responses. It will also make the finished guide easier to navigate.

Typical categories include the following:

- *Rationale and strategy:* Why the change is happening and how it meets business goals
- *Structural details:* What's changing, when, how much, and what's been done so far
- *The transition process:* How the change will happen (e.g., resources, activities, impact on ongoing work, plan for informing customers, suppliers and others)
- *Impact on the business:* How the change will affect revenue, customer service, competition, and other parameters of the business
- *Impact on individuals:* How the change might affect pay and career paths, how employees and others might benefit
- *Job transitions and development:* Layoffs, relocation, training, new positions, opportunities for transfer or promotion, changes in reporting structure
- *Sources of information:* Where to get help, who to contact for more answers, sources of career guidance, contact people

In the early stages of developing the FAQ guide, you are likely to have a significant number of questions that don't fit in any of the defined categories. Create an "all other" category to hold these questions. As notes accumulate, you'll see themes emerging from which you can build additional categories. Continue refining the questions, consolidating duplicates, and ensuring that the final set of questions are clearly stated, cover all the key issues, and overlap as little as possible.

PHASE 3: DEVELOP RESPONSES

Develop strong, concise, and clear responses. State the relevant facts briefly and accurately. Make them easy for everyone to understand—avoid jargon, function-specific terminology, and acronyms.[56]

Don't be afraid to state the negatives. People need to hear both sides of the story. Acknowledging problems or issues heightens your

---

56. Some acronyms (such as CRM, FY, SWOT, and TQM) are widely used and understood. But the countless acronyms specific to organizations often confuse as they abbreviate. A good rule is to spell out any acronym when first used. (To observe our own rule: customer relationship management; fiscal [or financial] year; strengths, weaknesses, opportunities, threats; and total quality management.)

FAQ guide's credibility.[57] Try role-playing to address difficult and complex questions. Use some trial and error, repeat responses and fine-tune answers until they're clear and concise.

It's likely that some of the questions from your brainstorming session will need to be answered by individuals outside the change team (e.g., senior executives; functional specialists such as IT, legal, HR staff). Use e-mail to deliver questions and ask for brief, clear responses. Specify when you need to receive these.

Focus on facts, not opinion or intent. Too often, responses in corporate FAQ guides sound like statements of intent ("We expect to gain market share by our commitment to strengthening quality and customer service") when they should provide real information that people can relate to and act on ("We expect to gain market share by offering a broader, higher-quality and more complete range of products than any of our competitors").

To help you create focused and informative answers, the templates starting on page 189 provide sample questions and responses.

One of the most frequently asked questions is: "How do we know this is going to work?" The typical response is: "We've worked hard to plan, and we're sure that this time we'll get it right."

In contrast, the sample response includes a list of solid reasons why the change will succeed. These include expanded training, new communication processes, employee involvement at the workgroup level, additional resources (such as added headcount), and other tactics. You can adapt the responses as needed based on your own strategies.

As you develop responses to complex questions, look for feedback from subject-matter experts and from stakeholders. Ask colleagues to read what's been drafted and suggest ways to strengthen the content.

Fine-tune the FAQ guide with thorough editing for consistency and clarity. If possible, include someone on your team who has strong editorial skills who will ensure clarity and consistency in all responses. Your aim is to enable the guide to work as a self-service support tool for employees and managers. If answers aren't clear and specific, it might raise more questions and concerns.

---

57. It's better to put the issue on the table and provide a comment, even if it's on the lines of "We're working on it and will have a response by . . ."

PHASE 4: TEST AND DEPLOY THE GUIDE

An extended review with a wider virtual team will enable you to test the guide, gain new perspectives, and build additional involvement to support the change. This wider team might include:

- ♦ People from other parts of the organization, anywhere in the world.
- ♦ People in functional roles that were not represented on your core FAQ development team.
- ♦ People who are indirectly involved but could offer valuable insights (e.g., customers, business partners, key suppliers).

In most cases, you can manage this process via e-mail.

As with your original review cycle with your own team, be sure to provide guidelines to the virtual team. For example:

- ♦ Invite reviewers to clarify answers—make it clear that you are looking for accurate and concise wording.
- ♦ Ask reviewers to contribute new questions (along with answers).
- ♦ Clearly state a due date when feedback should be returned.
- ♦ Explain briefly the plans for follow-up. For example, describe how the finished guide will be distributed, mechanisms for gathering feedback, and plans for periodic updates.

Once you have integrated the input from the extended review and refined the final draft, you're ready to distribute the FAQ guide to all those who'll need information about the change.

A typical distribution method is to post the guide on an internal Web page and share the link with everyone who might have an interest in the data. As you continuously update the material based on changes in plan or direction or on further input, be mindful to always post the latest version of your document. Alert people when an updated version is available to ensure they've got the most recent and accurate information.

Guidelines for driving useful feedback
Adapt the sample e-mail of reviewer guidelines to ensure clear and descriptive feedback. See Resource 6.5 (page 187).

If this approach isn't available or appropriate, you can distribute the FAQ guide via e-mail, in hard copy, or both. A subset of questions that specifically address issues for managers (e.g., pay issues) may be useful.

Let people know the FAQ guide is a collaborative, living document, with contributions from many people, and that new input is always welcome. Seek input from those who use the material to continue strengthening the guide to support a successful change.

See Resource 6.6 (page 188) for a checklist of tactics that can be useful for deploying the FAQ guide.

Case history: Supporting managers during change

A regional retail chain acquired a competitor. Though the deal was described (as they often are) as a "merger of equals," the acquirer was certainly the driving force and in control of the integration process.

A manager in the acquired business missed the meeting at which the merger was discussed, and her supervisor was out of town and unavailable. The manager had some concerns about the implications for her own job and career; and for the impact on her team. She needed guidance on how she should deal with the changes, and she was already fielding questions to which she didn't have answers.

She was referred to an internal Web page that included a detailed FAQ guide. She quickly learned that no jobs would be lost. But some of her other questions remained unanswered. E-mail sent to a link on the site generated a response within an hour from a member of the planning team, who addressed some of the urgent issues. Others, specific to the impact on her team, were referred to the still-traveling supervisor.

A day later, she returned to the online FAQ and saw that her question, in a generalized form, had been added, along with other issues raised in the discussion.

"They're listening and they seem to care," she commented.

The resource, and the response to her questions, contributed to her confidence in the process. When her supervisor returned, she was ready to talk about issues and direction, and to begin working on plans for managing the transition.

"Ideally, the process would have started with a conversation between me and my boss," she said. "But at least there was a resource that got me through the first 24 hours."

RESOURCE 6.1: MAKING THE CASE FOR AN FAQ GUIDE

These notes can be used in making the case for developing a FAQ guide to business leaders, and/or to encourage people needed to join the development team.

Purpose of an FAQ guide

The *[name of change initiative]* will have a significant impact on employees. How we deal with questions and concerns will be an important factor in managing the transition. An FAQ guide that addresses expected and actual questions with clear and specific answers can do the following:

- Provide a source for well-informed and consistent communication about the change.
- Help managers effectively support their teams through the transition with ready and accurate responses to common concerns.
- Motivate confidence and support for the change by demonstrating that the organization is aware of key issues and concerns, and is giving them careful attention.
- Support communication for sales, marketing, HR, and other teams who need crisp, clear answers about the change as they address customers, media, suppliers, and others.
- Serve as a focal point to attract additional questions (and answers) to keep the material current and relevant.

Benefits to managers

Managers respond to questions and address concerns about the change in the course of informal day-to-day meetings and conversations. Such interactions are an important part of the change process, and can be useful in identifying concerns as well as responding.

However, the volume and complexity of questions, and the number of people involved, make it difficult to address everyone's concerns and to do so consistently.

RESOURCE 6.1 [CONTINUED]

The FAQ guide will do the following:

- Save time and improve communication by providing a set of standard responses that are authoritative and accurate.
- Reduce the pressure on managers to address the questions of many individuals by providing a centralized forum that both employees and managers can easily reach.
- Support managers' concerns with a section devoted to issues of special interest to them, such as dealing with job losses or other transitions they will be managing.

Benefits to broader planning

The process of developing the FAQ guide will help with broader change management planning in these ways:

- Provide—through the development process—a forum for those involved in and affected by the change.
- Drive consistent messaging and reduce the need to repeatedly develop new materials.
- Exercise a forcing function—early in the planning process—through which we ensure that the case for change is clear, complete, and appropriate.
- Clarify for everyone the behaviors that need to change in order to ensure a successful transition, and to sustain or strengthen business performance.
- Help the organization communicate effectively with a compelling story about the change.
- Develop a foundation for building trust in the change process.

Benefits to team members

Helping to develop an FAQ guide provides an opportunity for team members to play a strategic role as well as a tactical one. As a team member, you will be able to do the following:

- Exercise influence in defining the change process.
- Demonstrate strategic insight and leadership in the way you approach the task and in the resulting document.
- Play a role that brings you in contact with key people at multiple levels of the organization.
- Use your own perspectives and experience to ensure that the document is adapted to the needs of your workgroup or team.

Use of the FAQ guide

The FAQ guide will provide managers, employees, customers, and other stakeholders with answers to many of their questions—and guidance on where they can go for additional information.

The content can be used as the basis for other forms of communication, and to focus attention and thinking on the change process.

Here are some of the ways in which we expect to deploy the guide:

- Distribute to the primary audience of managers and employees. A different version may be developed for each subsidiary, dealing with issues specific to that part of the organization.
- Provide the FAQ guide to communication managers and others, to serve as source material and ensure accuracy and consistency.
- Make the document available by placing it on an internal Web page with links to sources of information and guidance.
- Use the guide in training programs and other development activities supporting the change. This practice will provide consistent and clear messaging, and also offers another opportunity for developing new material and enhancing the product.
- Provide a Web-based version that includes an option for providing additional questions, and a section where managers can share ideas, tactics, and experiences that will be useful to others.

RESOURCE 6.2: INVITATION TO JOIN THE FAQ TEAM

This material is a template for following up after an initial call or e-mail. The purpose is to set out the goals of the FAQ document and expectations for team members.

Subject: Formation of an FAQ development team

Preparations for implementing *[name of initiative]* are getting started. I'd like you to join a team that *[name of executive]* has asked me to lead.

Our mission is to develop a set of questions and answers dealing with concerns and questions that may be raised. This FAQ document will provide guidance to managers as they address employee questions and will provide essential support to the change effort.

The date and time of our first meeting will be determined as soon as the membership of the team has been defined. Our intention is to hold the meeting within the next several days.

What's the commitment?

We have been asked to have the FAQ document ready for *[name of team or group]* review by *[date]*. This means that we have *[number]* weeks to complete our primary task. During that period (starting now), I'm estimating you'll need to commit about *[number]* hours each week to meetings, phone conferences, and e-mail communications about this work.

In addition, some team members will be spending time writing, reviewing, or editing draft material. Those commitments will be discussed and agreed upon at our first meeting.

After we deliver the draft, there will be a small continuing time commitment (perhaps an hour a week) to work on updates, integrate feedback, and respond to questions.

What's the purpose of the FAQ document?

The FAQ document will be used to guide communication, assist managers, and coordinate and align the work of the various teams working on implementing the change.

This material will be a consistent source of reference to guide the change process. We intend that it will also provide a focal point for generating further questions and ideas, and will go through revisions and updates to keep it alive and current.

It will be online, making updates easy to post and distribute.

RESOURCE 6.2: [CONTINUED]

How can I deal with my current workload?

If adjustments need to be made to your current workload to allow you to participate in this team's work, you should discuss that with your manager.[58] If this continues to be an issue, please let me know so we can explore ways of addressing it. *[Name]* has indicated that this project should be given high priority.

Have specific roles been defined for team members?

We'll define specific roles during our first meeting. We'll also share certain broad responsibilities, including contributing ideas and energy; offering perspectives that are representative of the various stakeholder groups involved; working fast and effectively to produce an effective, tightly edited summary document; and ensuring that we engage people widely in contributing ideas, information, and feedback.

[Add a personal note for each individual.][59]

I'll call you soon to discuss this, but don't hesitate to let me know if you have any immediate comments or questions.

---

58. The impact of change on workload can be a sensitive issue. A frequent cause of derailed change is the failure of the organization to recognize the extent and intensity of the added work (in addition to ongoing job demands) needed to plan, implement, and embed change.
59. For example: "Your contribution to this team will be invaluable. We'll truly value your understanding of the business issues involved, and especially your insights based on the changes you implemented in your plant last year."

RESOURCE 6.3: A MEETING FRAMEWORK FOR POWERPOINT

The outline below can be transcribed into PowerPoint as a starting-point for a slide deck that can guide an initial meeting for the FAQ development team.

1. [Title slide]
Topic of meeting; name of sponsor; date

2. Agenda
- Meeting goals
- Expectations
- Identify questions
- Clarify and classify
- Develop responses
- Edit for clarity and brevity
- Agree on next steps
- Assess the process
- That's it . . .

3. Meeting goals
- Develop a set of Frequently Asked—or Anticipated—Questions
- Draft responses and/or seek information and answers from the appropriate individuals and/or groups
- Plan deployment of the FAQ guide to ensure that it fulfills its function of providing clear, consistent, and accurate answers
- Define steps to assess the effectiveness and application of the guide, and to update and maintain it

4. Expectations
- Work collaboratively to identify issues and questions and begin to develop responses
- Ensure that everyone gets a chance to offer opinions, raise their own questions and offer suggestions: listen to all input and ideas
- Stay on track and recognize that some subjects can't be dealt with at this session
- Commit to carry out agreed follow-up work and continued collaboration

RESOURCE 6.3 [CONTINUED]

5. Identify questions
- Contribute any questions already compiled in the course of planning meetings or other discussions
- Identify issues and needs of specific stakeholders (including employees, managers, and customers)
- Generate as many questions as possible—no need or expectation to supply answers at this stage
- Record questions for later consolidation, clarification, organization and editing

6. Clarify and classify
- Review questions and group them into categories such as these:
  - ✓ Rationale and nature of the change
  - ✓ Business impact
  - ✓ Handling of job transitions (e.g., layoffs)
  - ✓ Career and development issues
- Continue to eliminate overlaps, consolidate similar questions, and edit for clarity and brevity
- Aim to have two simple questions rather than one complex one
- Use an "all other" category for hard-to-assign questions
- Review the "all other" group and identify additional categories that may need to be created

7. Develop responses
- Prepare clear, specific, and concise responses to as many questions as possible
- For key and/or complex issues, discuss and fine-tune answers until you have a brief yet clear response
- Where answers are unknown or unavailable, identify the individuals or groups who can provide them . . .
- . . . and define responsibility for seeking the input
- Agree on who will compile a first draft of the FAQ document
- Discuss steps for review, revision, deployment, and updating

RESOURCE 6.3 [CONTINUED]

8. Edit for clarity and brevity
- ♦ Refine answers to be concise and consistent
- ♦ Develop responses to complex questions . . .
- ♦ . . . and look for feedback in the process
- ♦ Ask colleagues to read what's been drafted
- ♦ Test responses on stakeholders
- ♦ Compile complete draft for review by team members and others

9. Agree on next steps
- ♦ Clearly define responsibilities:
    - ✓ Completing an initial draft
    - ✓ Reviewing and editing the material
    - ✓ Distributing the FAQ guide
    - ✓ Managing ongoing updates
- ♦ Establish timing commitments and review dates, including future meetings
- ♦ Determine sources of additional guidance and advice for questions that couldn't be answered
- ♦ Assign responsibility for gathering additional input
- ♦ Identify and resolve any remaining questions and issues about the team's process

10. Assess the process
- ♦ Plus (+)
    - ✓ What did you like about the session?
    - ✓ What should we repeat and/or build on?
- ♦ Delta (Δ)
    - ✓ What didn't you like about the session?
    - ✓ What would you change?
- ♦ Comments?
- ♦ Any other observations or ideas?

11. That's it . . .
- ♦ Many thanks—and see you next time

12. [Repeat title slide]

RESOURCE 6.4: TACTICS FOR BRAINSTORMING QUESTIONS

To help the team generate questions and ideas for the FAQ guide, it's helpful to do some creative brainstorming. The goal is to generate many ideas quickly, and then select the best ones. Following are suggested tactics.

Use role-playing to identify specific stakeholder concerns

Ask the team to think about the issues and needs of a specific group of stakeholders, such as employees, whose roles will be affected. Make sure everyone understands that this is not about answers—what you're looking for at this stage is questions.

Systematically focus on each stakeholder group and generate questions that members of that group are likely to raise. Repeat the process for each group who is affected by the changes and/or who is able to influence the outcome.

Throughout, encourage follow-ups and impose no limitations on topic or scope. Don't discourage negative and challenging questions.

Generate questions by systematically focusing on major issues

After an initial process of identifying topic areas, move from subject to subject and document questions within each area.

Spend 10 or 15 minutes talking about the rationale for change, for example, then similar time periods on other key topics (e.g., implications for pay, sales integration, IT).

Have each team member offer a few scenarios about change from the perspective of their own experience, and present questions they think would arise from people in those situations. The team can then add follow-up questions from there.

Open the floor to any and all issues

Encourage the team to ask the most challenging questions they can think of. The only criterion is that the question should be one that others will likely have.

Invite the group to offer the questions that they would least like to have to answer—the more challenging, the better.

Give people free rein—no restrictions or judgments, whatever comes to mind. At this point, quantity is more important than quality; there are no wrong ideas or "stupid questions." Remind the group that at this stage, you're looking for questions, not for answers.

RESOURCE 6.4 [CONTINUED]

Remember external stakeholders. Consider the implications in the marketplace, including how customers will respond.

Make sure you hear the participants' own questions

If you have a diverse group representing a range of stakeholder constituencies, then all their own questions will have relevance. Ask team members to express their own concerns, issues, and ideas—these will likely be shared by others.

Prompt discussion by asking what could go wrong, what needs to happen for the change to be effective, who will be most concerned, and who will respond most positively.

Do some of the work in subgroups

If you divide into subgroups, you can generate energy and creativity with multiple discussions, leading to a broader set of questions.

After an initial session with the full group, you can allocate three or four topics to each subgroup and have them focus on identifying questions around those areas.

Always ensure that each group (and the full team) maintains an "all other" catchall category so that no important question or idea is lost.

RESOURCE 6.5: E-MAIL GUIDELINES FOR FAQ REVIEWERS

The following is suggested text for a cover e-mail to send along with your FAQ guide when you distribute it to individuals outside the team for an extended review.

To: FAQ guide reviewers

The attached document is the draft of the FAQ guide for the *[name of change initiative]*. Please review this document and return your comments and suggestions to me by *[date and time]*.

This guide provides a comprehensive set of questions and answers that everyone can use as a reference for working through the transition. The FAQ guide will:

- ♦ Provide a source for consistent communication.
- ♦ Help managers effectively support their teams through the transition with ready and accurate responses to common concerns.
- ♦ Motivate support by demonstrating that the organization is aware of issues and concerns, and is addressing them.
- ♦ Support communication for sales, marketing, and other teams who need crisp, clear answers as they address customers, media, suppliers, and other stakeholders.

We are looking for specific suggestions that will strengthen the document. When you suggest changes or additions, please be as specific as possible. Avoid comments such as "this isn't clear" or "this needs to be rephrased"; instead, tell us what you think would make it clearer or more accurate. Remember that brevity is important. Please keep your wording concise.

As you review the document, note your changes using the Track Changes feature in Word (to activate this feature: from the Tools menu, select Track Changes). This helps us assess and integrate the input across multiple reviewers.

By *[date and time]*, we will make the guide available to everyone who needs information about the change. Updates will be posted at *[URL]*, along with other materials relating to the change.

Your input and guidance is much appreciated. Please let me know if you have any comments or questions.

RESOURCE 6.6: TACTICS FOR DEPLOYING THE FAQ GUIDE

Following are tactics to get the word out about your FAQ guide and build support for a successful transition.

Distribute to change sponsors and communication managers

Ensure that those who sponsored the change initiative are involved in the extended review (if they're not on the team itself). Seek their input on responses and new issues.

Direct the FAQ guide to the persons or groups—such as HR and marketing—who manage communication with key stakeholders (e.g., employees, customers, shareholders). Advise them to ensure that materials they distribute are consistent with the content of the guide.

Encourage feedback to strengthen the guide

Let people know that the guide is a collaborative, living document and that you welcome input and new questions (and answers). Seek input to strengthen existing responses.

Post the document on an internal Web page

Make the guide easily available by posting it online. Include the URL in all communications about change.

Keep the document current

As the change process evolves, new issues will arise, and other developments may modify existing answers. Keep the material updated. Maintain version control to ensure that everyone is referencing the most recent, accurate, and relevant information about the change process.

Stay connected to your team

Continue to work with your team on changes and additions to the guide.

Use the Web to solicit questions and best practices

On the internal Web page where the FAQ guide is posted, include an option for visitors to post questions. Include a "best practices" area where managers can share ideas, tactics, and experiences that will be informative and useful to others.

RESOURCE 6.7: FAQ TEMPLATE—THE CASE FOR CHANGE

This template includes sample FAQs and answers that focus on the rationale and strategy for a change—why things are changing. The setting for the example is the acquisition of another business. The templates in Resources 6.8 through 6.11 deal with other topics in the context of different kinds of change activity. Your own responses will reflect the status and activity in your own organization.

1. **What's the purpose of this deal?**

   Our goals are to strengthen our offerings to customers by expanding our product range, extending our geographic reach, and strengthening our service capability. Specifically, we will:

   ◆ Expand revenue by expanding new product and service offerings, and by adding sales offices in regions that we don't currently cover
   ◆ Increase productivity by integrating some of the systems and customer service processes that have made *[name of merging organization]* an industry leader

2. **When is this going to happen?**

   The legal details will be completed by *[date]*. The transition and integration process is expected to take 6 to 9 months.

3. **Why will it take so long?**

   There's a great deal of work to do to combine the two operations (with significant sales and manufacturing resources). We'll also have to work with customers to merge accounts, rationalize our many vendors, and build an integrated service and support operation.

4. **How will the process be managed?**

   We're forming an integration team to work out the practical details of plans and processes to make it happen. Primary tasks will include refocusing the product line, combining sales teams, rationalizing distribution, building an integrated IT system, and aligning compensation programs.

RESOURCE 6.7 [CONTINUED]

5. **Do we have to do this? What's the risk if we don't continue to make acquisitions?**
    We have a significant share of the market but don't yet lead in any segment; and we have incomplete geographic coverage. We're committed to making strategic acquisitions that will expand our product line to the point that we're leaders in at least half of the markets that we serve. Stepping back from this strategy would open us to the risk of being overtaken by more aggressive competitors.

6. **How can we be sure this deal will be a success?**
    The acquisition will be a win for our people and our customers— and for both businesses—for three primary reasons:

    ◆ First, both companies are operating profitably. The synergies of the merger will add to the total results in a positive way.
    ◆ Second, the cultures of the two organizations are very similar. Like us, *[name of merging organization]* believes strongly in focusing on the customer and on industry-leading quality and service standards. And, also like us, they value their people as the key to innovation, service, and growth.
    ◆ Third, the integration team—with people drawn from both organizations—has already made great progress in identifying key processes that need to be in place to support the merger.

7. **What will this really achieve for our customers and our people?**
    For our customers, the merger will mean a broader and more closely integrated product range with more service options. They will experience a faster response to issues relating to inventory, pricing, and product features. For our own people, the merger will mean enhanced opportunities in a larger organization, and expanded career potential.

8. **How will the deal address our current problems and needs?**
    Our current problems and needs were assessed by the integration team. Here are the top three issues that they identified, and how the change will address each one:

    *   *Incomplete product range:* We have been working hard to fill the key gaps in the product range (especially in consumer markets), and the acquisition will accelerate this process.
    *   *Limited customer support:* We have succeeded based on great product performance, but even great products need support, and that's an area where we need to improve. *[Name of merging organization]* has an industry-leading online support resource that we plan to deploy for our entire product range, across every region.
    *   *Career opportunities:* The slower growth that we've experienced in recent years has limited the opportunities for our most talented people. The merged organization will offer a broader range of career options to all employees.

9. **Will people not involved in the integration team have a chance to express their opinions and make a contribution?**
    Yes. Everyone in the organization is invited to check out the merger Web site at *[URL]* and provide input, including questions and ideas. In addition, the integration team will be directly seeking input from many people at all levels, functions, and locations.

10. **Our business is strong—why change?**
    Our business is strong, but our customers are developing new and different needs, technology continues to change, and our growth is slowing. We can't afford to stand still: we need to stay ahead of the curve, innovating, adding new products and services, listening to our customers, and creating new opportunities. The acquisition of *[name of merging organization]* offers an opportunity to address almost all of these challenges. If we pass up this opportunity, we may have to watch our competitors move ahead.

RESOURCE 6.7 [CONTINUED]

11. **What's the plan for implementing this change process and making sure it works?**

You'll find much more about the process at the integration Web site, including a summary of the business case and the approach to implementation. The integration team will be focusing on seven core areas where programs and processes need to be created or aligned to ensure the success of the combined business.

12. **What are the areas within the integration team?**

The integration team has seven main areas of focus, each with a group of people responsible for it:

- *Clarity:* Ensure that the strategic purpose and approach are clearly defined and described, and that people at all levels of the two companies understand and support the direction.
- *Engagement:* Build programs and processes to engage and involve key stakeholders, including employees, managers, and customers.
- *Resources:* Define and make available the resources (e.g., financial, human, physical) to enable the change.
- *Alignment:* Ensure that key systems and processes (e.g., reward, information, accounting, training) support the change; integrate and make changes to these systems as needed.
- *Leadership:* Put a strong team in place to lead and guide the process; ensure that leaders at all levels are committed to the change and able and ready to support and drive it.
- *Communication:* Continuously gather input from stakeholders; build processes to provide answers, share best practices, resolve issues, and act on ideas.
- *Tracking:* Put systems in place to assess progress, including the financial, economic, and human aspects of the change; follow up and make adjustments as necessary.

Several of the seven areas have subteams. For example, a subteam within Resources is working on IT/systems integration. A subteam of Alignment is working on reward systems.

RESOURCE 6.8: FAQ TEMPLATE—STRUCTURAL DETAILS

This template includes sample FAQs and answers that focus on the structural details of a change—what is changing, how it will work, where and when it will take effect. The setting for the example is the implementation of a new sales organization, with strengthened customer support and a shift to a single account manager for each customer. Adapt responses to reflect your own situation.

1. What are the main features of the change?

[Insert features from your change summary document—see Chapter 3.]

- ◆ Bring the four US regional sales groups and all customer-service operations into one organization.
- ◆ Continue and complete the outsourcing of hardware support to *[organization name]* while strengthening our own online and telephone service resources.
- ◆ Bring sales and support for each customer under the direction of a national account director in the same region as the customer's head office.

2. Are these changes worldwide?

This phase of the change process applies only to North American units. Overseas, we operate under a variety of different sales structures and processes; each foreign affiliate is now studying the market, the competition, and business needs, and will be developing new approaches. In many cases, they will be looking to us for guidance and leadership, based on our experience in the regional test and with the national rollout of the new model.

3. Who designed the new structure?

A *[name of team]* team with representatives from each region has been working on this for more than a year. They have invested heavily in the planning and assessment process, and involved many people across the organization. They also gathered input from customers and closely studied our competitors.

RESOURCE 6.8 [CONTINUED]

4. What has been done so far in terms of implementation? Has this been tested anywhere, and what did we learn?

The *[name of team]* team successfully launched the new account management model in *[region name]* last year. We learned a great deal about how to best manage the transition on a larger scale, including many helpful lessons on how to improve processes and strengthen communication. We learned that more time and resources need to be committed to building the sales-support teams under the new national account directors. We also need to emphasize training to guide all customer-facing employees on relationship management and business development issues.

5. When will this change go into effect?

The change will be phased in during the next *[number]* months. Team meetings will be held soon. During these you will have the opportunity to contribute to the detailed planning of the transition.

6. Are we done with restructuring for a while?

We're only done with restructuring if competitors slow the pace at which they're developing and introducing new products; or our customers decide they don't want improved support; or the marketplace stops evolving. Much more likely, these factors will continue to change and develop, and we will too, as we try to get ahead and stay ahead.

RESOURCE 6.9: FAQ TEMPLATE—BUSINESS IMPACT

This template includes sample FAQs and answers that focus on how the change initiative will affect the business—the impact on revenue and growth, and on competitive and industry status. The setting for the example is a major geographic expansion, but the content can be adapted to many types of change.

1. **What's the expected impact on profit margins?**

   Our profit margins have been declining, with intense competition, more customer price sensitivity, and our high support costs. The commitment to national distribution will arrest this decline by increasing our reach, expanding business with current customers, and adding new customers. And it's scalable—we can handle a much higher volume of business without proportionate investment in our distribution and sales operations.

2. **How will this affect our financial results?**

   Starting next year, we expect to see gains that wouldn't have accrued without these changes. This year, the investment of time and resources in the transition will have some short-term impact, and our financial forecasting is appropriately conservative.

3. **How will this strengthen the business long-term?**

   Greater customer responsiveness, increased customer satisfaction, higher sales volume, lower support costs, improved teamwork—these are just a few of the ways in which the changes will strengthen the business.

4. **Where will we continue to invest?**

   We'll invest wherever it's needed to continue to serve our customers and grow the business. In the near term, much of our investment will be in building resources in the expansion regions, preparing people for roles in the new organization, and ensuring that the new structure is fully effective. Looking ahead, we're beginning to plan changes to strengthen the support operation.

RESOURCE 6.9 [CONTINUED]

5. What other growth opportunities are we aiming to capture by this expansion?

Currently, our primary areas of strong growth are in *[product categories]*. In these areas, strong service and support are critical to keeping existing business and to adding new customers. But we also see opportunities outside our core business—in *[product category]*, for example. To capitalize on these opportunities and successfully sell into customer organizations with operations across the continent, we need national coverage for sales, distribution, and support.

6. How will this help us grow revenue?

We'll be adding new business that currently is going to competitors.

7. Won't there be heavy costs associated with the transition?

The costs involve training, building teams in the new regions, creating operating processes and resources for the national support organization, and many others. But the costs of not making the changes would be much higher in the long run, in terms of lost business and opportunities.

8. Couldn't the impact be negative, at least in the short term?

Yes. There'll be a short-term negative impact while we start to invest in the new structure and begin the transition. Thereafter, the impact will only be positive.

9. What are some of the major benefits of this change?

[Insert features from your change summary document or other materials.]

RESOURCE 6.10: FAQ TEMPLATE—TRANSITION MANAGEMENT

This template includes sample FAQs and answers that focus on the management of the transition, including questions about customer communication, employee and manager involvement, and internal communication. The setting for the example is a transition to a new solutions-driven sales model. Your own responses will reflect the reality of what's happening in your organization.

1. **Is the transition immediate or phased?**

   The changes will take about *[number]* of months to be phased in. By *[date]*, we expect the transition to be complete and that all customers will have been informed of the changes. More importantly, customers will be experiencing the changes as our sales teams begin to emphasize problem-solving and solutions.

2. **What should I be doing meanwhile?**

   For now, continue in your current role, reporting to your current manager, and working with the same customers. You will soon be invited to a transition planning meeting with your new sales-support team, and the national account director(s) for your customer(s).

3. **Will I have a new manager?**

   In many cases your manager will be the same, but there will be some reassignments to ensure we get a balance of skills and experience in each team.

4. **What will happen at the transition meetings?**

   At these sessions, you will be involved in defining and assigning account responsibility. Wherever possible, existing customer relationships will be preserved. You will also take part in planning how and when we'll communicate with each account about the transition to the new team.

RESOURCE 6.10 [CONTINUED]

5. What have customers heard so far?

Customers already know that we are planning to increase our emphasis on business problem-solving, provision of complete solutions, and a broader array of products and services to support those solutions. Many customers have been involved in formal or informal data gathering. Almost all have responded very well to questions about how we can better meet their needs.

6. Will we be meeting with every customer?

Yes. Planned transition meetings with customers offer a great opportunity for rebuilding or strengthening the relationship. We have a variety of pricing and other incentives to reward customer loyalty through the transition, and see the change as an opportunity as much as a challenge.

7. How will we ensure that customers feel part of the process?

We are planning a formal announcement to customers and to external media. This will be made on *[date]*, and account managers will be making informal calls on the day before stories appear in the press. We want our customers to feel fully in the loop and to be getting information in advance rather than from a third party. In most cases, this won't be much of a surprise.

8. Do we have the right plans and resources to make this work?

Yes, we do, and here are some of the reasons for our confidence:

- We've been planning this in detail for *[number]* of months—many of you have contributed to the process through a variety of committees and workgroups.
- We've learned many useful lessons from the pilot region and have integrated these insights into the change plan.
- We have a broad array of resources (information, training programs, incentives, systems) to drive and support the changes. See *[internal Web page URL]* for details on these resources and how you can use them.

9. **Do our managers have the skills and knowledge needed to make this work?**

   They do—and we're providing additional support to that key group with workshops and other resources that have already started. We're confident that they have the skills and knowledge they need.

10. **What training or other guidance are managers getting?**

    By the end of the year, everyone with a leadership role will have completed three one-day workshops on the new sales-support approach and structure, consultative sales skills, and management of sales teams.

11. **How is the overall transition being managed?**

    The integration team has seven subteams (see below). Representatives of these meet regularly to share results, ideas, and plans.

Subteam	Role
Business case	Build a concise summary of the case for change and the transition process; ensure that the purpose and approach are clearly defined and described, and that people at all levels understand and support the direction.
Stakeholder analysis	Engage and involve key stakeholders, including employees, managers, and customers; assess their concerns, ideas, issues, and needs; use results to drive transition planning.
Resource allocation and facilities integration	Define and engage the resources (e.g., financial, human, physical) to enable the change, including management of temporary staffing and other external resources; address facilities integration including plant relocation, closures, and consolidation.
System and process integration	Ensure that key systems and processes are fully aligned and support the change; areas of attention could include rewards, systems, finance and planning, HR (e.g., training, staffing, development), product-service integration.

RESOURCE 6.10 [CONTINUED]

Leadership and organization development	Put a strong team in place to lead and guide the process; ensure that leaders at all levels are committed to the change and able and ready to support and drive it.
Internal and external communication[60]	Continue to monitor stakeholder input; provide answers, share best practices, and resolve issues; ensure liaison with government and industry regulators; manage public and media relations and information.
Measurement and assessment	Put systems in place to assess progress, including financial, economic, and human aspects; follow up as necessary.

These subteams don't represent the only work on integration. Almost everyone will be involved in local, workplace discussions of how best to manage the transition. Everyone will play a role in getting the new sales model up and running quickly and effectively.

12. **What about employees in general? Are they getting help or support to get through the transition?**

There are a variety of programs available to employees. The Web page *[URL]* has information and guidance, and provides an opportunity to ask general questions. For questions relating to specific or personal issues, the first person to go is your manager or HR rep. If they can't deal with the issue, they can find the appropriate organization or person to help. In addition, town hall meetings led by VPs will be held in most locations. These will provide updates on progress, information about resources, and opportunities to ask questions and offer input.

13. **How will people move into the new roles in this organization?**

The move into new roles (e.g., for those moving from internal sales support to an external customer relationship role) will take place over the next *[number]* months. This allows time for careful preparation of customer transition plans, full implementation of the new CRM (Customer Relationship Management) system, and appropriate training for the people making the shift.

---

60. For example, government relations, corporate communication, and marketing.

14. Where can we go with questions about the changes?

If you have issues that aren't addressed by this document, please talk with your manager. And you can find the latest version of the FAQ guide at *[URL]*. On that site you can also enter your own questions or ideas—to which responses will be posted.

15. When can we get past all this and get back to the routine?

We have to learn to deal with continuing change. We can no longer establish a structure and set of processes and expect to leave them in place, unchanged, for several years. If anything, change will accelerate. We have to be ready to do what it takes to stay ahead of the curve. We want to be leaders in our industry—not followers.

RESOURCE 6.11: FAQ TEMPLATE—INDIVIDUAL TRANSITIONS

This template includes sample FAQs and answers about the impact of the change process on individual employees, including questions about how employees will benefit from the changes, how pay might be affected, and what career implications are expected. The setting for the example is a major reorganization and HQ relocation that includes some staff reductions. Adapt responses to reflect your own situation.

1. **What's in this for the average employee?**
   You have the opportunity to be part of a world-class organization, with industry-leading expertise, and a career path that can take you in whatever direction your interests and ability lead. Those who move to the new facility will have full relocation support.

2. **How will the reorganization affect my pay?**
   Salaries will be unchanged except for those moving to a higher-graded position. There will be opportunities for advancement, and the year-end review will evaluate pay in relation to new roles. Most employees can expect continued progression in line with their growth in skill, experience, and responsibility.

3. **What if I move to a lower-graded job?**
   For those few who move to a position that's graded lower, we'll freeze salaries (i.e., no reductions) until the range moves enough to enable an increase.

4. **Will my career path be affected?**
   This new structure offers good opportunity for growth. Talk with your manager about your own goals and how they can be met.

5. **What are we going to do during the transition?**
   Stay focused on doing great work for customers and colleagues. Work in alignment with our core values and practices. Support the transition however you can, but stay focused on your current role.

6. **Where can I go for more information about the change overall?**
   Visit *[URL]*—this site includes the change summary document and other planning documents, as well as points of contact.

7. **What do I do if I have questions not addressed anywhere?**
   We will be updating the online guide regularly, but if in doubt check with your manager or your HR rep. And please send further questions to *[e-mail address]*.

8. **Will anyone lose their job as a result of this change?**
   No jobs will be lost. We may need to hire in some areas.
   -or-
   As the *[names of divisions]* divisions are consolidated or phased out, we will be reducing staffing. HR will work closely with affected employees to help them find other positions in the organization. Where that's not possible, employees will receive a severance package. This will include service-based payments, job-search support, and guidance on extending health insurance.

9. **Will the other shoe drop? Will staff numbers be reduced again?**
   We have no current plans for further reductions, but can't state definitively that they won't ever occur. As with any other business, our goal is to operate profitably. We regularly update strategy and plans in the light of changing economic circumstances, and realign our structure as necessary. As markets, customers, and technology change, we'll continue to evolve and change in response.

10. **How is my new manager going to evaluate my performance at year-end if he or she has only worked with me for a few weeks?**
    Your new manager will be coordinating with your previous manager (and HR) to be sure they have all the necessary information about your goals and performance in the past year, as well as background on other issues that are relevant to your review, such as your skills, areas of expertise, and level of influence.

11. **How will we manage the increased transition workload?**
    Managers have been asked to assess their resource needs and the expected impact on their teams, and will closely monitor these issues as the change rolls out.

RESOURCE 6.11 [CONTINUED]

Employees may be asked to shift priorities and schedules to adjust workload, and in some cases to take on extra responsibilities until new staff can be hired. In those cases, appropriate pay and other adjustments will be made as needed. Where necessary, we'll use contractors or outsource some tasks.

12. What will be the process for filling open positions?

Managers have already outlined requirements for new hires (e.g., skill sets, background, training, experience). Wherever possible, we'll hire from within, either transitioning people between teams or engaging HR to help us tap into other parts of the organization where employees might be looking for new opportunities. Where openings remain unfilled, HR will work hard to recruit top-level talent into the organization as quickly as possible.

13. How will this affect each team's goals and results for this year?

Most employees will move to a new team. As these teams are formed, there will be a series of transition meetings at which goals and results for the year-to-date will be reviewed and discussed.

14. Will I have new goals?

We aim to ensure that all members of the organization go into their new roles with clear goals for the balance of the year. Their new manager will also be fully aware of their goals and contribution in the period leading up to the transition. For now, continue focusing on your current goals, but be ready to work with your new manager to redefine them.

15. How will people be assigned new roles?

For employees who are asked to move to a new position, managers have worked to match the right person with the right role. We want to align skills and expertise so everyone ends up in a fit that's good for them.

RESOURCE 6.11 [CONTINUED]

16. What if I don't want the position I'm offered?

If you're unhappy with the new role you've been assigned, you and your manager will work together to search and apply for a new opportunity in the organization. We'll try to move you to a role that best suits your skills, experience, and interest.

17. Will we train people who have to move into new positions?

A number of programs are available to support employee growth, from functional skills to leadership and team-building strategies. Work with your manager to identify the most appropriate training sessions for your role and desired career path. Your manager will also support any necessary rescheduling or reallocation of workload.

CHAPTER 7

At a glance

IF YOU NEED TO GET STARTED RIGHT NOW

This chapter provides an overview of the framework for the effective management of change. It includes questions to ask and tactics you can deploy immediately. Use the material here to assess status of a change initiative and identify needed action—to launch it, to move it forward, or to get it back on track.

The status of a change (planned, in progress, or complete) can be readily evaluated or tested by the questions—two for each of the seven core factors—that were introduced in Chapter 1. The questions explore the nature of the change; the extent to which it has been clearly defined and planned; the status and views of key stakeholders; the availability of appropriate resources for managing change; and other needs—many of which are often overlooked.

This chapter provides suggestions for actions within each of the seven core factors:

1. Clarity
2. Engagement
3. Resources
4. Alignment
5. Leadership
6. Communication
7. Tracking

Even local, small-scale change may present challenges and encounter obstacles. But continuing attention to these factors, and to actions that support and strengthen them, will go a long way to ensuring a successful transition.

1. CLARITY

In many change initiatives, the context, nature, and purpose of the change are not clearly spelled out for those involved and affected. This leads to uncertainly, lack of confidence, and inconsistent messaging and action. These, in turn, can derail change right from the start.

A clear summary document is invaluable. It can focus or refocus the purpose and process. It provides stakeholders with source material, tools for communicating with others, and guidance on how to provide support during the process. It provides a platform and framework.

Development of the document encourages or compels clear thinking about purpose and process. It ensures that leaders and others can readily and consistently respond to recurrent questions, including "Why are we doing this?", "How can we make this happen?", and "What does it mean for me?"

Core questions
- Are the purpose, direction, and approach defined and documented clearly?
- Are these understood and accepted by key stakeholder groups?

Tactics
- Develop a summary document to drive clarity, and to serve as a reference source on the purpose and process of change.
- Distribute the summary. Use it as a platform on which to build all communication (internal and external) related to the change.
- Create a brief elevator pitch for managers—what's changing and how the transition will be accomplished.
- Create other tools to assist in the process; for example, a brief PowerPoint presentation for executives and others to use while discussing the changes with their teams.
- Provide managers with talking points and suggested responses to key questions.
- Maintain and manage the summary. Seek input and comment; keep it current, accurate, and complete.
- Provide online access to the current version, and enable input, questions, and discussion.

2. ENGAGEMENT

Employee engagement can be described as an indicator of the degree to which employees feel committed to and involved in their work; the extent to which they are likely to commit their best efforts; and the likelihood that they will stay at their job and not look for work elsewhere. Engaged employees are more likely to be effective team members, and to support and drive change efforts.

Contributors to engagement include the work environment, team behavior, recognition, and involvement in work decisions and processes—a powerful tool for generating input, maintaining awareness of issues and opportunities, and moving change forward.

The extent to which managers connect with, listen to, and support their people is perhaps the primary driver. In the process of change, you need to prepare, engage, and support managers to communicate and actively lead their teams through the change process.

Core questions

- Have individuals and groups who can influence the outcome been engaged by becoming involved in the process?
- If so, have their input and ideas been acknowledged and applied to planning and action?

Tactics

- Support managers when they meet with their teams: provide discussion guides, talking points, FAQ guides.
- Emphasize employee involvement in planning and implementing the change.
- Train managers to build employee engagement through feedback, recognition, goal-setting, and support.
- Ensure senior leaders are visible and involved, and remain open to questions, ideas, and discussion about the purpose of the change and how it will be accomplished.
- Use face-to-face communication methods, including open forums and Q&A sessions, as well as ongoing meetings and other interactions among managers and employees.
- Identify key stakeholders and conduct an assessment about their concerns, questions, and ideas.

3. RESOURCES

Many change efforts fail because the needed resources (e.g., financial, human, equipment) aren't in place. Significant time and effort is needed to put change into effect. For example, new systems or organization structures may need to be developed; extensive training may be required for new systems or approaches; people may need to be selected and prepared to take on new leadership roles; many meetings may be needed to work out details of new business processes.

In short, managing change is an intensive process involving planning, analysis, communication, and discussion. There is a significant risk that attention will be diverted from day-to-day responsibilities—including serving customers. Amid ongoing work demands, the added tasks may take second place and be poorly executed or ignored.

Leaders therefore need to recognize that some projects or activities may have to be deferred if the change is to move forward effectively. Alternatively, additional resources for the transition period may need to be acquired from elsewhere in the organization, or from outside.

Core questions

- Are needed resources (e.g., financial, human, technical) in place and available?
- Is a strong and effective team in place and ready to lead and guide the change process?

Tactics

- Acknowledge the additional workload created by change efforts, and engage additional resources as needed (e.g., contractors).
- Facilitate adjustment of priorities to accommodate change, and provide guidance and assistance to managers and employees as they address the issues.
- Identify and acquire needed skills and resources (e.g., to undertake stakeholder analysis; to develop and document the case for change; to work on systems and process changes to align with and support the change).
- Make appropriate budget and other financial provision to ensure that resources can be sustained.
- Explicitly acknowledge and manage these costs as part of the overall process of change management.

4. ALIGNMENT

Alignment involves ensuring that business systems and processes collaborate in moving change ahead—or, at least, don't resist it. It may be necessary to modify reward systems, communication activities, training programs, IT systems, and other processes.

For example, a sales reorganization may call for significant changes to existing reward and incentive systems. There will be concerns and questions about these changes from the start, and a plan and process should be in place for addressing the issues.

Similarly, changes that have a major impact on one location or division need to be communicated across the organization. Employees and customers should be fully aware of what's happening; and aligned with the new structure, system, or approach.

Core questions
- Do systems and processes (e.g., rewards, information, accounting, communication, training) support the change?
- Have needed changes to these systems been identified, developed, and implemented?

Tactics
- Assess key processes to ensure that they support the change. These might include rewards (especially incentives), IT systems, accounting processes, and other administrative procedures.
- Add training and development programs as needed, to ensure that people are aware of and appropriately skilled in new processes or systems.
- Review and adjust communication processes and programs to be consistent with and to support the change.
- Support alignment by sharing information about the change across the organization, and not just in the areas affected.
- Continually seek input from stakeholders on systems or processes that may be impeding change, and that require work to create better alignment with the new goals and direction.

5. LEADERSHIP

Employees who are involved in change (but not leading it) often complain that they are being urged to behave differently while leaders seem to continue in old patterns.

Examples of needed new behaviors include promoting open communication, respecting and addressing work-life challenges, and focusing on customers. Leaders must ensure that everyone involved in driving the change—themselves included—are aware of behavioral expectations and are committed to fulfilling them.

For some change initiatives, new leadership may be needed to ensure success.

Core questions
- Are leaders at all levels of the organization involved in and committed to the change?
- Do leaders follow up on issues, provide guidance and support, and proactively manage the process?

Tactics
- Ensure that the primary sponsor(s) of the change (in some cases, and certainly for major changes such as mergers or acquisitions, this may be the chief executive) is visible, accessible, and consistently driving the process.
- Engage leaders at other levels in planning and implementation; provide guidance and training as needed.
- Encourage leaders to promote behaviors and actions that will support the change.
- Implement processes and activities to maintain leadership engagement—for example, weekly conference calls, regular e-mail bulletins, online forums, blogs and other interactive media.
- Address concerns that leaders may have about their roles and responsibilities in and after the change process: provide guidance, tools, and support.

6. COMMUNICATION

Communication problems are often cited as the source of issues and delays in change, although they can usually be readily addressed. Basic information about change is often lacking, yet relatively easy to provide.

Those involved in change typically have many questions and concerns, but they also have ideas about making it work. They need to be heard and engaged. Communication should be an ongoing, two-way process rather than a one-time or one-way supply of information.

This process is as much about understanding issues and needs as it is about providing information. Effective communication ensures that those leading change are aware of issues, questions, and concerns; and that their responses are provided in a timely and accessible way.

Core questions
- ◆ Is clear, timely, and complete information available to key audiences involved in and/or affected by the change?
- ◆ Do these groups have access to information, and a way of providing input and feedback?

Tactics
- ◆ Build an information framework around the business case or change process summary document (see page 67). Ensure that core data is available to all who want or need it.
- ◆ Include change-related information in existing media—and/or develop new processes to convey information (e.g., an intranet site focused on the change).
- ◆ Emphasize listening through formal and informal surveys, routine meetings and discussions, and ongoing manager-employee conversations.
- ◆ Continually update and revise resources (e.g., FAQs, change-summary document, guides for managers).
- ◆ Create a system—probably this will be online—to capture feedback and questions encountered by managers and others.
- ◆ Deploy social media to maintain a continuing flow of updates and brief reports or responses.

7. TRACKING

Follow-up is often forgotten in the pressure of day-to-day business. An assumption of success may permit problems to develop that can eventually derail change. Those involved expect and need support and follow-up. They want to be asked what's working and what's not. They need to be assured that their hard work and commitment are getting results and that change is helping the organization achieve its goals.

The process of tracking change involves gathering data about outcomes as well as seeking input from stakeholders about the impact on them and on the business. The questions yield responses that not only indicate whether the process is on track or not, but also indicate actions that can be taken to correct problems and address issues.

Accordingly, any assessment should include the opportunity for those involved to provide their ideas about needed changes and improvements, as well as a simple assessment of progress to date.

Core questions

- Are systems in place to assess progress, and to identify issues that need to be addressed?
- Are adjustments being made as necessary, and is information continuing to flow?

Tactics

- Conduct periodic surveys of stakeholders, exploring their experience with the change, its impact on customers and the business, issues that need to be addressed, and ideas for improvement.
- Include progress discussions in meetings on other topics. Keep the topic front and center until the change is fully accomplished.
- Maintain a focus on monitoring and course correction. Provide channels for feedback and ideas.
- Document questions and issues, and ensure that responses are developed and shared.
- Maintain communication among change sponsors so that problems can be recognized and addressed fast and effectively.

Glossary

This section describes some of the main terms used in *Changemaking*. You may find different descriptions in a dictionary or other source. With no generally accepted lexicon for change management, it seems appropriate to describe the usage in this book.

Agenda
List of items for discussion in a meeting or call. For long or multi-day meetings or conferences, the agenda may also include details of timing, discussion leader, and perhaps additional notes about the topic.

Alignment
The circumstance in which systems and processes (e.g., rewards, information, accounting, training) consistently support the change, and implementation is consistent and complete across the organization.

Assessment
A set of conclusions or judgments about a topic or process; for example, an assessment of employee attitudes to change could be based on a survey of employees. The survey is the process of data collection; the assessment is the resulting conclusions.

Breakout group
A process in which a conference or meeting is split into two or more smaller subgroups to work on specific tasks. The idea is to promote more effective discussion among smaller numbers of people, and also to enable multiple topics to be addressed in parallel.

Burning platform
A state of affairs that compels action. The phrase was coined by Daryl Conner[61] following a conversation with an oil rig worker who survived because he chose to leap from a burning oil rig into cold, rough water far below. It was an unattractive choice, but one that was forced on him.

---

61. Conner, *op. cit.*

Business case

Arguments justifying the planned action or change. The phrase is also used more broadly to refer to a document that not only makes the case for change, but describes the process through which it will be achieved.

Business planning process

The mechanism through which an organization establishes near-, mid-, or long-term plans. It may be ongoing though typically it's conducted in an annual cycle in parallel with financial planning or budgeting.

Change agent

A person or group who acts as a catalyst or champion for change; may not be the formal leader of the organization.

Change initiative

A planned action or set of actions involving part or all of the organization in significant change.

Change management

The set of processes, actions, plans, and decisions through which a change initiative is carried out and sustained.

Change-readiness

A measure of the extent to which an individual, team, workgroup—or entire organization—is ready and able to deal with change. A high degree of change-readiness might suggest, for example, that the organization and its people are flexible, are capable, have effective working relationships, communicate well, and can manage the resource needs often implied by change. An organization displaying low levels of trust, limited flexibility, and poor communication might be expected to have low readiness for change.

Checklist

A tool for assisting in planning and/or execution of a task by listing items that should be considered, planned, prepared, or conducted.

Climate, Organizational climate

The current status of employee attitudes, beliefs, and expectations. The climate may change quite rapidly based on circumstances. By contrast, organizational culture is the totality of experience, traditions, beliefs, and norms; and may be much more resistant to change.

Core factors

Characteristics or attributes that are associated with successful change. They include clarity, engagement, resources, alignment, leadership, communication, and tracking.

Course corrections

Actions taken to address issues and problems that arise during the implementation of change.

Culture, Organizational culture

Culture is used in the organizational context to describe the aggregate of norms, traditions, values, and beliefs. These forces strongly influence behavior, especially in the absence of specific guidance. The culture of an organization can be an asset or liability, and is generally slow—and sometimes difficult—to change.

Elevator pitch

A very concise summary of key points. The term is derived from the idea that in an opportunistic, informal discussion in an elevator or hallway, you may have 60 seconds or less to make a point. Even in more formal settings, attention span (in a meeting, discussion, or email) may be short, so the carefully thought-out elevator pitch can be a very useful tool for ensuring that the right messages are heard and retained.

Engagement

A sense of ownership and commitment; often assessed, in part, by measuring the intention of employees to remain with the organization and support its best interests. Involvement may be one part of building engagement.

FAQ(s)

Frequently Asked Question(s), often included in a FAQ document or guide as a resource for employees, managers, and others.

Focus group

A facilitated discussion among a small group of people who respond to questions and
discuss a specific topic for an hour or more.

Forcing function

A process that compels discussion and resolution of an issue. For example, development of a business case summary could act in this way by requiring goals and/or implementation plans to be clearly defined and described.

Guide (e.g., for managers)

A document or resource that provides guidance on dealing with a certain set of issues. For example, during change managers might receive a guide with a summary of the business case, FAQs to assist them dealing with employee questions, and suggestions on how they might facilitate a meeting of their teams to explain and discuss the process.

Leader

A person who directs and supports the work of others (e.g., leader of a team); person taking the primary role in facilitating a working group (e.g., a breakout discussion); person responsible for managing and facilitating a meeting or conference.

Levers of persuasion

Methods and processes through which people may be encouraged to support a certain decision or course of action. The levers may include discussion and argument, provision of information, demonstration, involvement in planning, rewards, appeal to the emotions, prevalent opinion among peers and others.

Plus-delta assessment

An approach for an informal assessment of an event, meeting, or process. The term derives from the two questions asked: "What went well and what did you like?" (Plus); and "What could we do better or differently next time?" (Delta). Responses to the first question open up discussion and encourage constructive responses to the second.

Sponsor

The individual or group who initiated the change. The change leader may be a different
person (or group), assigned the task of implementation. In many cases, especially in smaller organizations, the sponsor and leader are the same.

Stakeholder

Individuals or groups who will be affected by the change, and/or who can influence the outcome. Examples include employees, customers, stockholders, managers, supervisors, media, government, communities, labor unions, competitors, suppliers, partners, and many others.

Virtual team

A working group that may be widely dispersed geographically and that rarely or never meets face-to-face. Instead, members communicate by phone, e-mail, or other Web-based resources.

Index

Acknowledgements

I've learned about change, communication, and leadership from many people and organizations. My early experience was at Lever Brothers in Warrington, England, managing a plant producing more than 1,000 tons of washing powder every week. This was a powerful first lesson in how organizational performance depends on the way people are engaged, led, and rewarded.

Later in my career, leading Towers Perrin's communication consulting practice through a period of major change was another intense and invaluable experience.

I owe thanks to many at TP, including Roger D'Aprix (now a colleague again at ROI Communication), Glenn Bonci, Peter Bugbee, Joanne Dietch, Julie Foehrenbach, Philip Freud, Rodney Gray, Liz Guthridge, Jim Hanley, Pat Milligan, Suzanne Peck, David Rhodes, Susan Robboy, Diana Salesky, Alan Schnur, Mark Schumann, Jeffrey Seretan, Jim Shaffer, Rollie Stichweh, Sheryl Turping, and Anne Vitullo.

The International Association of Business Communicators (IABC) provided many opportunities for professional and personal growth. I must single out Brad Whitworth, with whom I worked when he was IABC chair and I was the board member focusing on international development. He represents countless other committed, thoughtful, and supportive IABC-ers.

Teaching at the University of Washington provided a wonderful opportunity (and the requirement) for me to organize and document my ideas and experience. Students in my MBA and Executive MBA classes brought fresh insights and were always ready to challenge and expand my thinking and approaches. I'm especially grateful to Professor Charles Hill for inviting me to develop and teach a course in the Executive MBA program, and encouraging me to expand the focus from organizational communication to the management of change.

I've been fortunate to have worked with organizations of every size in many industries. Since starting my own consulting practice, my clients have included AT&T, Avanade, Group Health Cooperative, Microsoft,

Nellcor (now Covidien), Penford, the Port of Seattle, and ASRC. These organizations have provided opportunities to work on many facets of organizational change and communication. John Cairns, Jeff Cook, Mike Creamer, Laureen DeBuono, Lori Dewey, Melissa Hawkins, Joanne Harrell, Jan Hjortshoej, Susan James, Annalee Luhman, Vic Okerlund, Diane Rondeau, Cathy Ryan, Simone Reynolds, and Michele Tringali are just a few of the many people with whom it's been a pleasure to work.

Don Summers and Chris Cardwell have been colleagues with whom I've collaborated in a variety of ways, especially on communication and leadership development for organizations experiencing and creating change. They contributed greatly to the development and documentation of my ideas and approaches.

My thanks to Luis Gonzalez, founder and president of Elliott Avenue Associates. He opened new doors and helped me realize (insisted, as a matter of fact) that I was far from ready to retire.

I much appreciate my association with ROI Communication and the opportunity to work with ROI's inspiring CEO, Barbara Fagan-Smith. Her energy and passion encourage me to keep working, learning, and teaching. How better to combine these than by writing a book?

When I began to translate some of my ideas and experience into material for others, Nick Allison, Ed Crawford, Phil Davis, Bruce Finley, Brian Grant, Bill Hurley, Gavin James, Judith Lawrence, Merry Phillips, Mike Smith, and John Ward were among those who offered especially thoughtful and useful insights and guidance.

Nick Allison gets a double mention because of his superb editing. His work turned a compilation into a book. Eric Larson advised me tactfully and entertainingly about book design. Bill Greaves designed a striking and effective cover. Kyra Freestar and Connie Chaplan dispelled my lifelong belief that I could proofread my own writing. The advice of these experts was invaluable, but errors, inconsistencies, and design or editing failures are of course my responsibility.

Changemaking is dedicated to my wife, Lesley Burvill-Holmes. Her understanding of the demands of a career that routinely calls for unsociable hours, schedule changes, and frequent travel has been extraordinary, and deeply appreciated.

Richard Bevan
Seattle, Washington

About the author

Richard Bevan was educated at Oxford University and Manchester Business School. After early experience in manufacturing management, he worked for Towers Perrin (now Towers Watson) in Europe, Australia, and the US, including five years leading the firm's worldwide communication consulting practice.

In 1995, he started his own firm, C2K Consulting, advising clients on organizational communication and change management. He was also an external faculty member for the University of Washington Executive MBA program, where he developed and taught a course in managing change. The approaches that he has developed and applied as a leader, consultant, and educator have provided the framework for *Changemaking*.

Richard Bevan lives in Seattle. In addition to his family, his non-business interests include cooking, sailing, biking, tennis, travel, reading, and gardening. In 2010, he managed to combine more than half of these pursuits in a sailing trip across the Atlantic Ocean from St. Lucia to the Azores in which he was responsible for provisioning and cooking. As well as *Changemaking* and the book that resulted from that voyage, *The Galley Slave's Handbook*, he has published a wide variety of articles, mostly on change-related topics.

He has been a regular speaker at forums such as the Conference Board and International Association of Business Communicators (of which he is an accredited member). He currently serves on the Board of Advisors for ROI Communication and as strategic communication advisor for Elliott Avenue Associates.